Growing UpCountry

Growing UpCountry

Raising a Family & Flock in a Rural Place

by Don Mitchell

Camden House Publishing, Inc.
A division of Telemedia Communications (USA) Inc.

Library of Congress Cataloging-in-Publication Data
Mitchell, Don.
        Growing upcountry : raising a family and flock in a rural place /by Don Mitchell.
             p.   cm.
       ISBN 0-944475-18-3 (softcover)
        1. Mitchell, Don—Homes and haunts—Vermont. 2. Novelists,
American—20th century—Biography. 3. Sheep ranchers—Vermont—Biography. 4. Vermont—
Social life and customs. 5. Country life—Vermont. I. Title.
PS3563.I75Z467   1991
813'.54—dc20
(B)   91-12135
                                    CIP

Designed by Eugenie S. Delaney
Illustrated by Carl Kirkpatrick

Camden House Publishing, Inc.
Ferry Road
Charlotte, Vermont 05445

First Edition

Printed in Canada by
D.W. Friesen & Sons
Altona, Manitoba

Trade distribution by
Firefly Books Ltd.
250 Sparks Avenue
Willowdale, Ontario
Canada M2H 2S4

To Anaïs

Other Books by Don Mitchell

Thumb Tripping

Four-Stroke

The Souls of Lambs

Moving UpCountry

Living UpCountry

Author's Note

Thanks to quirks of fortune and personal temperament, my family and I live without a camera and, therefore, have no photographic record of our progress and our projects here in the congenial wilds of Vermont. Writing a monthly magazine essay, however, became a way for me to keep an album fashioned out of words. I urge readers to approach these pictures of our life in the spirit with which they would browse a neighbor's family photos, and I hope that a comparable pleasure may be realized.

Grateful thanks is offered to my editors and friends at *Boston Magazine*, where these essays were first published in slightly different form. And to my intrepid, long-suffering wife, Cheryl. Most of all, though, to my children, Ethan and Anaïs, whose tolerance for having stories told about themselves has been more than generous. I expect they'll pay me back in kind, one of these days.

Perhaps it is true, in Tolstoy's famous phrase, that happy families are all alike. *Ours* has been happy in its very own way, however, and the four of us look back on episodes of life together that must surely be unique. I am pleased to have the chance to share them with so many others.

Contents

Creative Thinking

A fundamental fact of life in places like rural Vermont is that we are thrown back repeatedly, endlessly, on our own resources. Whether at work, at play, or at such simple tasks as trying to stay sentient as winter lingers on into March and April, we tend to depend less on a social fabric and more on *ourselves* to direct our aspirations, reward our achievements, and correct our mistakes. No surprise, then, that rural folk are known for their cussed independence. Their crustiness. Aloofness, even. Since our conversational skills are somewhat atrophied, we can be taciturn to a point that seems like insolence. But we deserve to be equally famous, too, for mastery of creative thought. Our problem-solving skills are continually honed by our being forced to do things for ourselves. Somehow. One way or another. Right now. By gosh or by gum.

Children are well served by being raised in an environment where they depend mainly on themselves for amusement and for maintaining an interest in life; kids who are self-starters surely never suffer from boredom. After generations of natural selection, the offspring of New England rustics may be pre-adapted to lives of self-reliance. It is not surprising to find children, out here in the sticks, wielding creative powers that can put adults to shame.

Take the simple matter of what toys a child plays with. I remember my son, Ethan, at the tender age of three, throwing himself on the floor of the toy department at a Ben Franklin store because he wanted to have everything. Impossible, I told him. Next came a stage when he'd wake up in the night, worried that some particular truck or doll or set of blocks on the store's shelves had been sold—the last one!—and no more would be arriving from wherever toys came from. My wife, Cheryl, and I did our best to tell Ethan about mass-production, trying to convince him that his fears were groundless. But from his perspective of rural isolation, it seemed all too plausible that Ben Franklin might run out.

In time, he learned to shield himself from these anxieties by dreaming up his own toys and making them with his own hands. Elaborate puzzles and games became his specialty—puzzles that no one but he could put back together, and games too complex to be played more than a couple times. No matter. *Making* these diversions had been their real point. Next time he felt like playing, he could make another game.

When Ethan was five, his sister, Anaïs, was born, and he immediately set about making educational toys for her—an enterprise that busied him for several years. He made toys to help her learn to read and write, so she would never have to know the worst pangs of boredom. Toys to teach her numbers, so she'd always be able to count anything she wanted. And toys to teach her how to make her *own* toys—all by herself—so that her joy in life could never be held hostage by the local five-and-dime.

For better and for worse, the creativity that rural life has nurtured in our kids has made them extremely hard to fool. While not entirely immune to the mythologies we offer them, Ethan and Anaïs prefer to invent their own. They can eye the world around them with cold objectivity, or—when they choose—they can invest it with the sheerest flights of imaginative meaning. Often as not, they can fix things when they break. They can teach themselves new tricks. One could do worse than to grow up way out in the sticks.

Fairy Tale

One of the sweeter, slightly more bizarre chores of parents is to perform the offices of various mythological beings: Santa Claus, Easter Bunny, Tooth Fairy. Children grow up paying homage to this wacky pantheon, and otherwise-rational grown-ups do their level best to shield their charges from the knowledge that it's all a hoax. One loses one's innocence in many small ways on the road to maturity, but surely Finding Out About Santa Claus is right up there with far more dangerous, more celebrated exploits.

Some, perhaps, have puzzled over the cultural utility of those supernatural entities. I used to wonder, too, until one spring day when the high psychological purpose of the Tooth Fairy started to crystallize in my thinking. Cheryl and I had penned our whole flock of sheep in the barn to "mouth" the older ewes, and Anaïs—then just six years old—had tagged along to play with the baby lambs.

"Mouthing" sheep means opening their jaws to assess dentition. Since sheep, just like humans, replace baby teeth with permanent ones, the progress of dentition in a younger ewe is one way to determine age. After four years, though, a sheep has acquired a "full" mouth; from that point on, things can only go downhill. As teeth gradually get worn down—or chip, or break, or just fall out—the animal's grazing efficiency begins to suffer. Eventually, this affects lactation ability, body condition, and basic metabolism; by the time an older ewe can be pronounced "a gummer," the cumulative effects of tooth loss may have reduced her to a walking cadaver.

The reason for mouthing sheep, then, is to annually identify animals in dental trouble, in order to cull them from the flock before they are discovered in some cold, rigid posture. So there we were—grabbing each of eighty ewes in turn, jotting down ear-tag numbers, and scoring each mouth on a scale of one to five. Across the barn, Anaïs delighted herself by chasing lambs around their grain trough; after a while she left them and climbed several wooden hurdles to join us in the sheep-examination pen.

"That's about a four," I told Cheryl.

"Want to black-tag her?"

"I don't think we need to yet. She looks good for one more breeding."

Anaïs moved closer to investigate our sober business. "What are *those* for?" she asked, eyeing the box of blank, unnumbered ear tags dyed the color of night.

"If we think a sheep needs culling, she gets one of these. We can turn her out, then, till we have a full truckload. It won't be any problem finding her later."

"What is culling?"

"Taking them to market."

"You mean killing, right?"

"Yes, I guess that's what I mean."

"Why?"

"Because—well, it's on account of their mouths," I told her. "Here, just look at this—" I caught a ewe who looked quite palpably advanced in years and spread her lips open to let Anaïs peer inside. "One missing tooth, there—right up in the front, you see? And this side tooth feels loose—look at this, it even wiggles! Now, when this sheep tries to bite off blades of grass, she's going to have a hard time. She could even starve, maybe—and she certainly isn't going to thrive on pasture. So it just makes sense for us to—"

"*I* have a loose tooth," Anaïs announced with uncertain pride, baring her upper gum and wiggling a baby canine back and forth.

"Honey—good for you!" laughed Cheryl. "Soon you'll be getting a visit from the Tooth Fairy!"

I stood waiting for the other shoe to drop—for my daughter to inquire if I planned to cull her, too. She was too polite to ask; the question seemed to resonate, though, in the awkward silence that ensued. Then I pointed out: "That's a *baby* tooth you're losing. You've got a brand-new, *permanent* tooth behind it, pushing the old one out. But this sheep has started to lose permanent teeth, and so—"

"Aren't there any dentists for sheep, or anything?"

"No."

Anaïs's upper lip began to tremble in the first early-warning sign that tears were on the way; she turned and climbed a final hurdle to escape the barn. As I squeezed the pliers to insert a black tag in a white ear, Cheryl put the clipboard down and followed our unhappy girl. We see little point in shielding our kids from the realities of farm life; still, a timely hug can go a long way toward helping children accept what is involved in husbanding commercial sheep. Working on alone, I reflected on the complicated attitudes we try to teach—to care for these animals the best we can but somehow keep our sentiments in check. No room for toothless sheep.

Anaïs's tooth came out a couple mornings later, and by that night it was dawning on me that this routine event of bodily growth carries with it a disturbing message of mortality. Even happy, well-adjusted children catch a whiff of it. Here was a bone that used to be inside her body—part of her skeleton, helping her chew her food—and now she could roll it, blood-stained root and all, between two fingers. *Sheep are made to disappear for precisely such bad luck,* I thought I could hear her thinking…or was I just thinking *for* her? One small step toward dust, or back to dust— the ancient, fundamental cycle. So I did the obvious: I kissed my little girl and told her, "Hey, terrific! Now aren't you excited? Put that underneath your pillow before you go to bed tonight, and first thing in the morning you will find a big surprise!"

Usually Cheryl does the Tooth Fairy gig at our place, but since these symbolic concerns were looming large for me—me, the good shepherd with a bent for triage—I volunteered to wear the metaphoric wings this once. I discussed the going rate, then set aside two quarters on a shelf in our closet. I even wrote a little note to wrap around the coins: *Glad to see your grown-up teeth are coming in so beautifully—and right on schedule, too! Much love, T.F.* Then, adult life being what it is, I plumb forgot to get up in the night and tuck these presents underneath my daughter's pillow.

Came the dawn, next morning. There are sins of omission for which parents can offer good excuses; forgetting to play Tooth Fairy, though, is not one of them. With the first gray light, Anaïs slumped into our bedroom in a sour mood. "You know what?" she whined, her small voice thick with disappointment.

"What?" I answered, groggy.

"The Tooth Fairy never came last night."

"Huh?" I heard Cheryl ask. "Are you sure?"

"I guess she forgot about me."

Waking up fast, I rolled over and said: "Gosh, that's odd—why don't you just crawl into bed with Mommy, while I check for myself."

"I already looked beneath my—"

"No Tooth Fairy? That's awfully hard to believe—I mean, there must be some mistake." Quickly I rolled out of bed, grabbed the note and coins, and went into my daughter's bedroom. There, beneath her pillow, was the lonesome-looking tooth. I scrawled a hasty postscript to the Tooth Fairy's missive—*Been a busy night, but I finally got here!*—and folded it up with the quarters tucked inside. Back in our own bedroom, I adjusted my best poker face and asked Anaïs: "Are you *perfectly sure* you looked?"

"Yes."

"Funny—because there seems to be something there now. I mean, I just saw—"

She threw the covers off and went back to investigate. I sighed with relief.

"Just about blew that, didn't you?" hissed Cheryl.

"I forgot!"

"Right. Way to go, Dad."

"Anyway, at least she'll—"

But Anaïs ran back in. "The Tooth Fairy came, all right, but you know what? She forgot to take my tooth!"

My wife pulled the covers up over her head, then groaned. I asked, my voice alive with interest: "Is she *supposed* to take the tooth?"

"She *always* does."

"She always does," Cheryl surfaced to confirm.

"Well, gosh. Imagine that. She must have been really busy last night, and just in a terrible rush, and—"

"I think I want to write a letter to the Tooth Fairy," announced Anaïs in a cold, litigious tone, as though threatening a consumer complaint. "I'm going to tell her that she'd better come right back, because my tooth is still underneath my pillow. Right where I left it."

"Good idea," Cheryl affirmed. "You go find some paper, and I'll help you write a letter." Then, once Anaïs had left the room, she fixed me with an outraged stare. "Forgot to take the tooth!"

"Sorry," I said. "I didn't know. It's been a long time, since I—"

"Taking the tooth is the entire point!"

"I see," I said. Things *were* becoming clear: since lost teeth are potent symbols of mortality—and nowhere more than on a farm with aging livestock—the purpose of the Tooth Fairy is to assure their ritual disappearance. To redirect the child's mind away from death, toward happy thoughts. And—bingo!—couldn't Santa Claus serve a similar purpose, livening up the cold, dark trough of winter solstice? Couldn't the Easter Bunny mitigate, for kids, the disturbing iconography surrounding Jesus' crucifixion? What better device than happy, mythic, gift-bearing spirits to divert our children's attention from the void?

Anaïs came back in with writing tools, and I did psychic penance by forcing myself to listen to her dictate while Cheryl wrote:

> Dear T.F.:
>
> First you didn't come, and then you came but you forgot my tooth. How come you forgot how you're supposed to do it? Anyway my tooth is still there waiting, if you could get around to coming back. I don't want it.
>
> Your Friend,
> Anaïs

Then, while my wife and daughter were discussing where to mail this complaint, I left the bed again and flushed the tooth down the toilet. This, too, turned out to be the wrong move. When I returned after doing the deed, Anaïs had just decided to enclose the tooth in her letter to the Tooth Fairy. Business-by-mail, see? All was forgiven—even Fairies, she had now decided, sometimes make mistakes. With a sinking feeling, I watched her tiptoe out to check beneath her pillow for a third time in just twenty minutes. In an unsuspicious world, I suppose she might now have wondered at the Tooth Fairy's quirky, inefficient, but ultimately thorough ways; instead, Anaïs came back with her jaw set in an attitude of all-too-grown-up skepticism. "Well," she said, "it's gone now."

"Great news!" I crowed, trying to spin things my way. "You mean the Tooth Fairy finally—"

"Sure," she answered coolly. "Unless you took it."

I counted on time to heal this wound. After all, given the choice between the Tooth Fairy and *nada*, what six-year-old can long resist the cheerful lie? I underestimated, though, the ability of farm life to nurture a depressingly objective outlook; farm children come to value cunning and craftiness and human ingenuity over the bland comforts of credulousness. And so, one morning four months later, when Anaïs announced at breakfast that There Is No Tooth Fairy, she seemed more excited with the thrill of her discovery than a visit from the sprite could have possibly provided. Still, I encouraged her to carefully reconsider. "*Everyone* believes in the Tooth Fairy," I began. "Because everybody knows that—"

"Dad—look!" she interrupted proudly, baring her upper lip and showing where a tooth had been.

"You've lost a tooth!" said Cheryl. "When did that happen?"

"Five days ago! But I just didn't *tell* anybody, so you wouldn't know! And that tooth has been tucked beneath my pillow for *five whole nights,* and—nothing! So that *proves* it, right?"

"Proves what?" I answered woodenly.

"That there isn't any Tooth Fairy, really. It's just you and Mom."

"Good detective work," laughed Cheryl, capitulating. "Scientific, too—first you formed a hypothesis, you made up an experiment—"

"Can I still have two quarters?"

"For your tooth?" I shook my head. "Absolutely not! But I think maybe it's time you started getting an allowance. Fifty cents a week, maybe—you think you're old enough for that?"

"Yes," she said.

"Well, I do, too."

I fished a couple quarters from my pocket, placed them in her hand, and noted that a kind of milestone had just been passed. Cheryl said: "Maybe you should *earn* your allowance, though. By doing certain chores."

"Such as?"

"Change your sheets and pillowcase, for starters—and while you're at it, *please* throw out that tooth!"

"All right," said Anaïs, getting up and [...]
staircase with a controlled grace, a studied ease that [...]
childish. Head aloft on shoulders that could bear the we[...]
Cheryl and I caught each other's astonished eyes: our Fairy[...]
over.

Explorations

Walled in by granite cliffs to the south and east, our farm seems no more likely to be invaded from these compass points than, say, Switzerland. As a happy consequence, we never fear waking up some morning to find ski chalets positioned along the ridges that define our view. The terrain is far too rugged; even hikers seldom go there. Several years ago, though, as I worked with two professional carpenters to frame the walls of my solar dream house, the rhythmic singing of our hammers became punctuated by frantic, childish screams emanating from the south cliff, a good quarter-mile away. Our valley had been penetrated.

Since the cliff is shrouded by thick treetops rising from the valley floor, there was no way for us to see the cause of this wild keening. When a dog joined in, raising its voice in a hysterical, unearthly howl, it seemed all too likely that some tragic miscalculation had resulted in a child's fall, somewhere on the rocky face. We could plainly hear the cries echoing off the cliff, borne our way on fluky breezes in the crisp morning air. "Help! Oh, help!" shrieked a little girl. "It's Casey!"

"Get up, Casey—*please* get up!"

"Oh my God, Casey—can't you even move at all?"

Dropping our tool belts, the three of us sprinted toward the farm pond. We dashed across its earthen dam and then, starting to lose our wind, jogged more slowly up into the forest at the south cliff's base. Soon we were scrambling over car-size boulders, climbing toward the sheer rock face. Finally we came upon four sobbing children, two of whom I recognized as neighbors from a nearby farm. They stood grouped around a puppy—a Labrador cross whose name turned out to be K.C. The

essly to catch some cliff-dwelling bird
ped off a precipice and fallen a good

, into my pickup truck, and over to the
ιe morning—three man-hours of labor,
r in cash. I wasn't angry, though. My
f sheer relief: I kept reminding myself it
easily *could* have been, so I gave the kids
f roaming steep terrain without a grown-
ιe, each one properly contrite.

This ɑrɑmɑι— f the issues of risk versus joy in childish exploration happened, for better or for worse, before my own kids began to show much inclination to wander about the farm. Until fairly recently, "going out" for Ethan and Anaïs meant playing within a radius of one hundred yards—no further—of our house. They were seldom out of sight, and they were always within earshot. The day did come, though, when I stepped onto the porch to call the kids in for supper, only to find that they had extended their range to points unknown. I shouted myself hoarse, then stalked back into the kitchen.

"Not around?" asked Cheryl.

"Vanished. Think we ought to worry?"

She laughed. "You're *already* worried, aren't you?"

"Yes, I am. I don't like this one bit."

"Just think back to when we bought the farm," she reminded me calmly. "We talked about what fun it would be for kids here. Growing up explorers."

"Yes, I know, but—"

"You said it could be just like the Hundred Acre Wood, remember? Christopher Robin and Winnie-the-Pooh? Or like *The Wind in the Willows.* Or like Tolkien. You said children could make up imaginary kingdoms here. Fairylands. Don't you remember?"

I did recall once expressing such sentiments on behalf of unborn children, but that had been years ago. Nearly half my life ago—before I'd even had a chance to *meet* the kids involved! Fairylands? Imaginary kingdoms? Looking back, these seemed just exuberant expressions of my own youthful idealism, pipe dreams of a young man who had not yet come to realize the terrible fragility of everyone and everything. "There are *cliffs* here," I pointed out with grim maturity. "Swamps—and maybe even quicksand. Leeches. Snakes. There are trees too weak for climbing. Porcupines and skunks and—"

"Well, kids need to learn about that stuff. So just relax, okay?"

Anxiously scanning the horizon out the kitchen window, I spied Ethan and Anaïs emerging from a corner of our distant woodlot. They ambled homeward, sporting slender walking sticks and apparently absorbed in animated conversation. When they stomped into the mudroom, I managed to greet them nonchalantly. "Where have you been?"

"Death Woods," Anaïs answered happily.

"*Death Woods*?"

"Where you dumped those sheep skulls and bones and stuff," Ethan said. "Remember?"

I blanched. "Yes, I think I do."

"Well, we're making a museum out there."

Every livestock farmer needs a private boneyard—a remote, well-protected place in which to dispose of the occasional animal who expires before it can be gotten to market. Flesh rots quickly during much of the year, helped along by worms and carrion beetles and turkey vultures; within days, a luckless lamb is usually picked clean—right down to its white bones and plastic ear tag. I had such a boneyard, except now it was no longer well protected or remote. In fact, it was becoming part of a museum. "What *kind* of museum?" I inquired.

"Natural history."

"I'm not sure it's smart to—" but I caught myself. Clean bones. There was no harm, really. Next time something died, I would take the trouble to bury it. "Wash your hands—*with soap*," I charged them. "Then sit down—it's suppertime."

A couple weeks later while I was working in the forest—er, in Death Woods—thinning a hardwood stand and simultaneously harvesting firewood for winter, the chainsaw heated up. I shut it off and as I started walking home to get some tools, I noticed a pine board nailed to a distant tree. Detouring, I read a childishly lettered sign: BONEHENGE.

An arrow pointed uphill to my left. I followed it to an outcropping of rock where half a dozen skulls lay arranged in a druidic circle, as though caught up in some grave discussion—say, group therapy. Shaking my head in wonder and bemusement, I turned around and headed back toward home. Maybe the museum hadn't panned out quite as my kids planned; still, they had found a way to use those skulls to create a striking sense of place. Having turned their imaginations to that corner of the forest, they had transformed it into a landmark in some private world.

Back at the house, while I rummaged for my chainsaw files, I noticed that several basic tools were missing from the steel box in which they are kept. Hammer, ripsaw, brace and bit, cat's paw—all had disappeared. Vanished. I called for the kids, but they were not around.

On the bulletin board where we leave each other messages, I found a note in my daughter's hand: Gone with Ethan to Happy Dancing Meadow. She might as well have written Gone to Moon. It was *my* farm, and I knew it well—knew every foot, most likely—but how was I to know where Happy Dancing Meadow lay?

Come suppertime, I asked them for directions. "First you go through Finger Forest," Ethan told me matter-of-factly. "Then you have to cross the Land Where the Sun Rises, circling behind Great Swamp."

"Great Swamp," I nodded. "I know where you mean. The thing is, kids, I don't think it's *safe* to play around Great Swamp."

Anaïs pulled a long face. "You only have to hike around the back of it. Then you come to Sacred Spring, and after that you climb until you're up on top of Bald Rocks."

"Bald Rocks?" Now I knew exactly where she meant: she meant a granite lookout on the east cliff's mottled summit. "You've been climbing up there?"

"Sure, Dad—that's the way to Happy Dancing Meadow. It's in the forest up behind Bald Rocks."

I shut my eyes, shuddering to picture my pretty ones dancing off some precipice. "You mean you two have been climbing up to Bald Rocks, and I didn't even know?"

"It's perfectly safe—you don't have to worry about a thing."

"It is absolutely *un*safe, and as your father I forbid you to—"

"But Dad! We're building our Indian Village up there!"

"*What* Indian Village?"

"Where we're going to have our camping trip. You and Mom can even join us. You should see the view from up there."

Now a new thought crossed my mind. "Have you been taking carpentry tools up to Happy Dancing Meadow?"

"Sure. You can't build an Indian Village without—"

"*My* tools?"

"Look, we only borrowed them—okay? We're going to bring them back as soon as we're finished."

"Tools *rust*," I told them heatedly. "You can't leave tools outdoors, in the open—it can ruin them."

Anaïs blinked back the tears welling in her blue eyes. Ethan yelled: "You're against everything, aren't you?" I shut up and let Cheryl handle the situation.

Cheryl is an excellent arbitrator. After supper we all climbed to Happy Dancing Meadow with a Styrofoam ice chest in which the kids could safely store my tools. And I had to give the kids credit for finding a route up the cliff that was gradual and never downright scary.

The "meadow" was just a grassy clearing in the scraggly, stunted forest atop the ridge; Indian Village was nothing more than a couple of half-completed tipis. But not in the eyes of my children. So far as Ethan and Anaïs were concerned, herds of wild buffalo roamed just beyond the copse of scrub pines. Medicine men scoured this craggy ridge for healing herbs. Smoke signals could quite easily be sent from here to forge alliances with neighboring tribes. As dusk began to settle I followed my kids down the mountain, intensely aware of the thirty-odd years between us.

Having thus established their right to roam anywhere on our widespread premises, Ethan and Anaïs set to work, steeping the entire farm in something like mythology. They even drew a map, at my request, to help Dad navigate his way around the kingdom: King Seat, Queen Seat, Gothic Arches, Woodland Cottage, Fairy Cliff, Bowl of Stone. By now, I'm sure there are many more imaginary sites. When I walk the woods either to ruminate or to size up timber, I feel the constant presence of a shadow world layered over what I consider to be my real one. If I stumble on a little cairn of stones, it *means* something. I have no idea what, but it could not have arisen without my children's design and purpose. If I find a rotting branch lashed between two trees, it may be some make-believe creature's sylvan chinning bar. Or some giant's towel rack. Or the ridgepole to a future hut.

Every forest testifies to nature's careful artistry; ours has now become a powerful example of the pleasures of imagination, too. Just the other day, mowing hay along the woodlot's edge, I noticed a pewter vase perched atop a moldering stump. Shutting down the tractor, I walked over to find a bouquet of wilted trillium poking from the vase's throat. On the mossy forest floor, a little purse lay open with a rhinestone necklace emerging from its zippered pouch. Behind the stump crouched a velveteen puppy dog with white, fluffy stuffing oozing from one leg.

Finding such tableaus in the woods does not surprise me now, but that puppy caused me to think back to the day when I had scolded kids from up the road for exploring. No child had slipped and fallen, after all. Children may not always enjoy magical protection, but between the ages of roughly five and fourteen they seldom willingly self-destruct. Properly nurtured—reared with grown-ups' loving care but offered a long leash of authentic trust—a child's bent for exploration ought to help *develop* caution, rather than the sort of curiosity that killed the cat. I considered heading up the road to offer a belated apology; I realized, though, that by now the children I had scolded had turned into young adults. Teenagers. And that, as they say, is a whole different story.

I am *still* impressed with the fragility of all I cherish. Cliffs make scary playgrounds, and a rural landscape such as ours is fraught with perils every bit as dangerous, in their own way, as those which urban environments afford their young. But I am growing comfortable with my children's explorations. There are certain risks to growing up, and I accept that so long as my children are willing to accept that too. The payoff is more than just aiding the growth of what I hope will be resourceful, independent personalities; the payoff is also the joy I take in getting to live—at *some* level of cognizance—in a world my kids created and are actively creating every time they step outdoors.

Where do they go? Out, somewhere. What do they do? Everything. With a little luck, they may teach me to keep exploring, too.

Rural Isolation Drills

Private elementary schools are few and far between in places like Vermont, but my kids have had the opportunity to attend one—the Bridge School, which occupies a converted dairy barn just north of Middlebury. Among other aspects of an estimable educational philosophy, Bridge School fosters a sense of humor. Students are encouraged to play complicated pranks on their teachers, who in turn come up with elaborate responses to keep their charges quick-witted and amused.

I remember picking up the kids one wintry afternoon and hearing Ethan tell me they had spent the morning taking part in a Rural Isolation Drill. "Oh?" I said innocently. Cabin-fever doldrums were certainly on the rise, but this seemed a peculiar way to help young kids address them.

"That's right," said Anaïs, straight-faced. "R.I.D., for short."

I put the family pickup into four-wheel drive and crabbed across the icy parking lot toward the highway. "And exactly what is a Rural Isolation Drill?"

"Sort of like a fire drill," she answered uncertainly.

"Not exactly, though," explained her brother. "First they told us that the government had declared us a Certified Rural School in a Designated Rural Area. So in case we had a terrible blizzard or something that would cut us off from the outside world, we had to be prepared."

"Like if the telephones weren't working," Anaïs offered. "And no radios, or anything."

"In city schools, you know how they have bomb scares?" continued Ethan. "Kids there have to do evacuation drills, but out here in the country, we don't need those. Instead, the government makes us do an R.I.D."

"What is it they made you do?"

"We put on coats and hats and went outside, and we had to shout 'Help!' all together—at the top of our lungs—into a machine that measured it. In decibels. To see how loud we all could shout. Then, after we got loud enough, the teachers made a tape recording."

"To send to Washington," Anaïs added soberly.

"Good idea," I said. "Anything else?"

"We had to lie down on the playground and spell out H-E-L-P in the snow. With our bodies. And we had to do it without any teachers helping out."

"What was *that* for?"

Wide-eyed, Anaïs answered: "In case airplanes or helicopters up in the sky might be looking down, and then they'd find us. They could drop down food and games and stuff, so we wouldn't have to starve to death or get too bored."

"And the teachers all climbed up on the roof," Ethan continued, "and they took a lot of photographs to send off to the government. To prove that we knew how to make our bodies spell out H-E-L-P, even without grown-ups showing us how. We had to spell it big enough and clear enough so the government would know if an airplane pilot could look down and read it."

"The government in Washington, D.C.," Anaïs reiterated.

"And then they told us that the main thing to remember," said Ethan, suddenly modulating his voice, "was that the entire Rural Isolation Drill was a great big joke!"

"What did you do then?"

"We just lay there in the snow, laughing and laughing," said my little girl.

"Of course," said Ethan, "you never know when something like that might come in handy."

Indeed. As parents raising children in the wilds of Vermont, Cheryl and I have routinely wondered how various forms of "rural isolation" may be shaping our kids' youthful personalities. Their nearest playmates, for example, live at least half a mile away; the nearest athletic field is six miles away. It's not that we don't have abundant open spaces, but nearly all of it is dedicated to growing crops and grazing critters. Kids like ours know how to climb rocks, catch frogs, and build a tree house; they would not know what to do with roller skates, though—or with tennis rackets, for that matter—even if they owned such items, which of course they don't. Someday, when they first encounter squash courts or lacrosse sticks, they will be amazed at the range of sports about which we told them nothing.

Things are worse than that, however. Most rural parents—like most modern parents everywhere—rely on television to enlarge their offsprings' understanding of the world and to simultaneously perform low-cost babysitting services. From TV, rural kids learn that they live in an essentially urban nation, fraught with urban dangers, and that most other children have a host of concerns that are truly unfamiliar. Such as how to safely cross the street, how not to get lost downtown, and how to avoid a host of Faginesque characters and Dickensian temptations.

TV also offers kids a shared mythology, involving such iconographic figures as Miss Piggy, Cookie Monster, and The Smurfs. Can a child grow up "normal" while remaining unaware of this arresting cast? And, of course, TV indoctrinates children in our secular religion of shopping, of consumption, of Going To The Mall; out of such shared values is our cultural identity currently forged. But *our* rural household, in a gesture of breathtaking isolationism, has not possessed a television set in a dozen years.

It was one of the bitterest battles in our early days of parenthood, and I lost it—utterly. Cheryl, whose career is in childhood development, flatly refused to have "one of those boxes" within our infants' field of vision. TV, she maintained, fosters in children a disturbingly passive attitude toward entertainment. I *knew* that, I protested, but a little passivity can be fun, now and then. I suggested: Love me, love my television.

No, said Cheryl. That thing goes or *I* do.

For a brief time we compromised by keeping "that thing" in a closet; after the tuck-in hour, I could drag it out and tune in the odd program. Children, I solemnly promised, would not be exposed. Soon enough came the Sunday afternoon when I got busted: Cheryl came home from a grocery-shopping foray to find young Ethan in the living room with me, watching football. True, he was as interested in exploring the *back* of this strange machine as in regarding the gladiators doing battle on its screen. But I had gone back on my word, and I knew the consequences.

Others may—others *did*—consider the loss of my television as evidence of henpecking. But my wife maintained that living without The Tube was simply a corollary of the Thoreauvian ethos that had brought us to Vermont in the first place. Having voluntarily detached ourselves from mainstream culture, why allow its values to be broadcast into our home?

Now, some twelve years later, I feel sure Cheryl was right. Children raised without TV *do* assume more active, resourceful attitudes toward entertainment...and toward how they spend each waking hour. They're more inclined to read and write and draw and make up their own games. They tend to sing more, and dance and play musical instruments. They're much less likely to be obsessed with growing up; they *like* childhood because they can live it fully.

A screen did eventually come into our house, but it belonged to a computer. Cheryl and I had some early fears that this wondrous tool would get our kids hooked on games like Zork and Wheel of Fortune—games that are by no means inherently stupid, but which restrict one's mental efforts to following where another mind has been. Our misgivings were unnecessary. Ethan lost interest in playing the standard computer games after only a couple times. He studied how they *worked*, however, so that he could make his own. At the local library, he borrowed half a dozen books and taught himself to program—God knows, *I* can't do it. Now, at fourteen, he has a dozen floppy disks filled with his own computer games that *other* children come to play.

So, for our growing family, rural isolation has had certain costs and benefits. Of course, I can't help wondering whether these kids are being adequately prepared to live someday in urban milieus, should they ever choose to. In the worst case, I worry that they'll find themselves dead meat: unsuspicious, overly trusting, bright-eyed innocents abroad in an evil world. Still, any young person's ingenuous qualities are easily lost and damn hard to regain; perhaps the longer my kids can hang onto theirs, the better off they'll be. And the nicer grown-ups they'll become.

A few weeks after the Rural Isolation Drill, I went to a parent-teacher conference to discuss my kids. Arriving early, I browsed about the Bridge School's meeting room; there, on a bulletin board, were glossy photographs of the school's entire student body lying on the snow-covered parking lot. The camera angle, taken from atop the old barn's roof, was rather oblique—not the perspective that would be afforded to a pilot flying overhead. But the message was wonderfully garbled all the same: P-L-E-H. One or two organizational types were still running around, trying to rearrange their classmates' bodies and arguing, no doubt, about which direction airplane pilots read from.

My daughter's teacher strode into the room and greeted me. I said: "I was told these photos were going to be sent to the government. In Washington, D.C."

"Total failure," he assured me amicably. "Better that we just not tell anyone down there. But we're so isolated, I don't think they're going to miss us."

"*My* kids don't have any sense of rural isolation," I protested cheerfully. But in the same breath, I couldn't help thinking: if they *did* become fed up with the odd conditions of our life here, now I knew exactly what my kids would try to do. They would march out in the snow and send a call for PLEH! As Ethan had assured me, you never know when skills like that are going to come in handy.

Batter Up

A couple years ago Anaïs learned to ride a bicycle, but there were few destinations that Cheryl and I felt she could ride to safely. The hilly, winding, two-lane road that runs past our farm is plied by all manner of speeding vehicles, up to and including eighteen-wheel tanker trucks that haul our neighbors' milk to Boston. Viewed from the cab of such a rig, small children riding small bicycles must appear no larger than the skunks, raccoons, and porcupines whose run-down carcasses litter our rural highways.

Fortunately, our house is set back from the road by a rather long driveway. Eight hundred feet long, to be exact—enough for a proud girl to imagine she is heading somewhere when she sets off, wobbling, on her bright two-wheeler. The terminus of her ride is our rural mailbox, mounted atop a six-by-six hemlock post that pokes from the shallow ditch that drains the road. She can stop there by the mailbox, dismount, and check for new communications from the outside world, then ride back to the house and file her report.

These intelligences had a certain boring, either-or consistency until the morning when Anaïs burst into the house to say that the mailbox had been smashed.

"You mean someone hit it?" I asked, hiding my dismay.

"It's all dented in—come see!"

She rode, and I trudged behind, as we traversed the driveway to its intersection with the road. Of course I knew she wouldn't lie, but I kept alive the hope she might have been exaggerating. Sadly, she was not. The galvanized steel box had been dealt a crushing blow, crumpling its hinged door into the surrounding metal and even thrusting its supporting post five inches out of plumb.

"Damn," I said, and for once my use of what Anaïs calls "a swear" went uncorrected.

"Maybe someone's car went off the road," she suggested.

"I don't think so."

"What, then?"

"Well, it may mean someone doesn't like us much."

"Who?"

"Just some kids, most likely. I don't know who. This is what people in the cities call *vandalism*. Or malicious mischief."

"Why would kids come smash our mailbox?"

"Well, maybe because—" but I found the issue far too complicated to explain. How the gentrification of our rural society, fueled by a growing horde of immigrants from out-of-state, has displaced the landscape's natural heirs by driving up living costs beyond the means of natives and even further beyond any means that the natives' kids seem likely to attain. How young people frozen out of real estate markets, rental housing markets, and skilled-employment markets might direct their anger toward anyone perceived as an outsider. How does one explain that to a child?

"Will we have to buy a new mailbox now?"

"Listen," I proposed. "Let's take this one into the shop and see if we can't hammer it back into shape."

"Okay."

Half an hour later, the mailbox had reassumed something of its classic shape; its door, too, could once again be opened and shut, albeit with some difficulty. We mounted this symbol of our family's identity back on its post, then drove into town to buy new stick-on letters to affix to the box, spelling out MITCHELL. Funny thing: 100 yards down the road, we passed the remains of our nearest neighbor's mailbox. Blasted to smithereens. It had been molded of some tough, high-impact plastic, but whatever struck the thing had caused it to explode. A little farther up the road, we passed the next mailbox—a modern, decorative affair styled like a red-and-white hay barn in miniature. It, too, was smashed. Next came an exquisitely handcrafted wooden mailbox, a scaled-down replica of its owner's house. Thoroughly demolished.

The road from our driveway into town is seven miles long, and— to make a long story short—on that morning there appeared to be not one single undamaged mailbox. Whatever miscreants had bestirred themselves the night before, one had to admit they were completely catholic in their taste. Maybe they weren't much in favor of outsiders, but the Vermonters on our road who could pass any test of genetic purity also found themselves with no way to receive their mail.

The hardware store, needless to say, was doing a brisk business. *New* mailboxes, at fifteen bucks apiece, had completely sold out. Small hinges for remounting the doors of salvageable mailboxes were nearly gone. Metallic paint was going fast, as well as sundry other items. I gave Anaïs the job of picking out our stick-on letters, while I joined in conversation with a heterogeneous group of rural crime victims.

"Kids today," said one. "Always out running the roads, and all this celebrating. What have they got to celebrate about?"

"Just figure up the damage those kids did in one night! What do you think—one hundred mailboxes? *Two* hundred?"

"Couple thousand dollars' worth of mailboxes, easy."

"In one night!"

"I don't suppose it took them all night," drawled one older man whose eyes still bore a glint of youth. "Might have taken no more than half an hour."

"How?"

"Kids call it mailbox-baseball. One guy drives along in a pickup— fast—and his buddy sits behind him in the bed with a baseball bat. Three strikes and he's out, you get it? Then they have to switch positions."

"*This* guy didn't miss a swing," I said. "So far as I can tell."

Anaïs brought the letters M-I-T-C-H-E-L-L over, and we marched together to the checkout counter. As a young woman rang up the purchase, I overheard a final scrap of conversation from behind me: "What if we all get our boxes fixed, and then those kids come back?"

Sure enough, they did—and not five days later. Our rural community is not so closely knit as it once was, but we voiced a collective groan of embattlement the following Thursday morning when, once again, every mailbox from Weybridge to Vergennes had been soundly whacked. This time I did not need to suggest to Anaïs that the vandalism had in any sense been aimed toward *us*. It had been directed toward society at large, spilling from some reservoir of sheerest anomie. Every last residence along our peaceful road, from the lowliest trailer to the most expensive country home, had a newly busted mailbox.

And then, scarcely before the paint had dried, it happened *again.*

Vermonters are so unaccustomed to crime—let alone to faceless, gratuitous attacks on personal property—that this third attack was widely construed as an all-out assault on civilized values. Ordinarily kind, gentle, mild-mannered folks began to threaten staying up all night, shotguns poised and loaded, waiting to blast the "baseball" team. Others spoke of schemes to fill their mailboxes with explosives that would detonate upon a bat's solid impact. Even aging peaceniks like myself pondered whether life-without-parole was a stiff enough sentence to impose on mailbox bashers. How could our society permit such delinquents to roam about at large?

Someone may have tipped off the perpetrators that a dozen contracts had been put out on their lives, for the attacks ceased for several weeks. During this hiatus, some remarkable refinements were made to mailboxes up and down our road. A common early style of defense was to erect some sort of shield on each side of the box, interfering with a batter's hypothetical swing. Shields were composed of strips of spring steel curling skyward from a mailbox's post, or lengths of two-by-eights spiked together in a criss-cross pattern, or—eventually—thick, cedar gateposts rammed into the ground on three sides of a mailbox, shrouding it with a miniature stockade.

I took note of each new ingenious solution to the problem of defense but declined to take action. My instinct for deviant psychology suggested that the mailbox smashers would only feel challenged—"Hit Me!"—by such obvious measures. And, sure enough, they were. After the fourth attack, neighborhood consensus was that the players must be swinging not a Louisville Slugger but an eight-pound sledge.

This crisis—and it *is* a crisis when each household has to mount a new mailbox four times in a couple months—eventually brought out the deepest creative strains in people living on our road. One man suspended his box from a trellis with wire so fine it would snap off at first contact and drop to safety. Another man took a welding torch to fabricate a mailbox out of three-eighths-inch steel plate. It *looks* just like a mailbox, until some vandal tries to hit it. Then—well, as he said, "I hope that meathead breaks his arm."

Several citizens along our besieged road altered the entrances to their driveways, moving the mailboxes far back from the shoulder. Our patient Letter Carrier now turns off the road to reach them, but speeding pickups fly on past. Less-well-heeled types began routinely taking in their boxes every night and setting them back out each morning, adding to their daily chores. The niftiest solution I came across, however, was a large rural mailbox lined with foam rubber and hiding a smaller mailbox inside. The outer shell could be dinged all night, I imagine, without the slightest damage to its inner sanctum.

I give my daughter credit for our solution, which emerged only after replacing our first mailbox once and being on the verge of replacing the replacement. Driving to the hardware store, we went past example after example of creative vandal-proofing. Anaïs said: "You ought to fix up something so those guys *think* they're smashing our mailbox, but they really aren't."

"A decoy, huh?" I might have cried, 'Eureka!' By the time we pulled into town, our plan was fully formed: we bought a new, small rural mailbox, took it home, and sandwiched it between our two hopelessly dented big ones. Now, no matter what direction the delinquents come from, they see a looming target and can have their satisfaction. Next morning we still have an intact receptacle in which to receive our mail.

The character of rural life *has* been changing, recently; I have even heard that some of my neighbors lock their doors at night. In twenty years, who knows what the neighborhood will look like? Anyone who drives our road, though, checking out the mailboxes, will see what well-worn traits Vermonters rely upon as they face an uncertain future: stubborn pride and pluck and unbounded ingenuity. Watching my Vermont-born daughter riding her two-wheeler up and down our long driveway, checking on the the mail, I like to think she's going to fit this culture admirably.

Provisioning

If classic New England farms can be viewed as little kingdoms, then their farmers must, from time to time, feel like little kings. I have known this feeling. While I have no subjects to rule over except sheep, who will not listen, and two kids, who have learned to answer back, and while I have no armies or servants to command, my farmerly ability to sculpt the local landscape does confer regal satisfactions. Performing this work takes a lot of time and effort—more, perhaps, than any real king would care to undertake—but then it also keeps me out of trouble. On balance, it's a good deal.

My experience of life here has been kingly in another way. As many fairy tales of courtly life make clear, kings can be prone to bouts of king-size depression. The ruler slouches on his throne, golden crown askew; jugglers and jesters and dancing maidens find themselves helpless to improve their liege's stinking mood. A latent rage often accompanies such melancholy; after all, if anybody ought to have the means to achieve sustained happiness, shouldn't a potentate? Or, indeed, a farmer— since all farmers have the daily option of asserting themselves upon their kingdoms in ever-new, creative, satisfying ways.

The exercise of such Faustian energies *can* be a tonic for depression, I have found—once one gets one's kingly derrière in gear. At such times, I try to think of some new activity I wish we could do here on the farm—and *would* be able to do, if only things were different. Swimming, for example. When the urge to have a place to take a dip became overwhelming one hot summer, I managed to find a bulldozer jockey willing to swap fifty hours of pond-digging for fifty breeding ewes. Soon the vista from our house embraced a broad expanse of water.

Then, a few months later, when the newly filled pond seemed imperfect for lack of a beach—a place to spread a towel and sunbathe, read the Sunday paper, and watch the kids build dikes and castles—I snapped my regal fingers and made several groaning truckloads of sand appear. I spread some of this along the banks of the pond; later, in mid-winter, I spread a lot more sand atop the pond's skin of ice so that, come spring thaw, it would drop to the bottom and cover the sticky clay where we wade in to swim. Why, after all, should rural kings have to emerge from their ablutions with muddy feet?

There was still something missing, though. For a time I thought it might be a summer house—a delicate gazebo down by the water's edge for summertime frolics. So I built one—no big deal, in terms of either time or money—and, for a while, my appetites were satisfied. Not for very long, though. There was still something missing—the means to some joyous pastime that had brought me hours of sheer pleasure in my boyhood. All at once, it came to me: I wished that I could crouch down

by the pond's edge, pick up flat, smooth stones, and skip them out across the water.

But I *had* no skipping stones down at the pond—nor, I figured, anywhere else about the kingdom. Acknowledging this deficiency was depressing. There was the young prince to consider, and the younger princess—what kind of a childhood would they have if their natural environment afforded no stones to skip?

Elsewhere on the place I kept a shallow pile of gravel, which we mined occasionally to mix batches of concrete. I sifted through this stash of coarse aggregate one morning, in search of likely skipping-stones. Slim pickings. Oh, there were some rocks that could be made to bounce a few times—maybe—but I found absolutely none of the flat, smooth, silver-dollar-size stones that can be made to kiss the water fifteen times or more, performing graceful, gravity-defying dances before sinking to the bottom. I doubted that such stones could be ordered by the truckload, and even if they could be, I realized in a philosophically tough moment that purchasing them would take the sport away. Perfect skipping-stones need to be stalked, discovered one by one, sized up, and hefted individually by the hand that plans to toss them. Otherwise, it's just too easy.

Our farm is rather self-sufficient, recreationally; those of us who live here almost never feel the need to travel anyplace else to experience the great outdoors. It happened, though, a year ago, that I had to visit a Vermont State Park some twenty miles away, on the shores of Lake Champlain. The park's summer ranger does a bit of custom butchering in the off-season, and I wanted to engage his services to transform some fattened lambs from on-the-hoof to in-the-freezer. After pinning down a couple of slaughter dates, I took a little walk to explore this manicured domain which had been placed in his care. Wandering down a steep, shaley path to the water's edge, I suddenly found myself in stone-skippers' paradise.

Much of Lake Champlain is firmly rock-bottomed, and at various places the lakeshore is quite rocky, too. But here, lo and behold, the rock had a layered, sedimentary character that seemed to be steadily breaking apart, helped by the action of waves and the endless freezing-and-thawing cycles of our climate. At any rate, I was standing on a rocky beach strewn with thousands of smooth, flat stones that looked eminently suitable for skipping. Some of them were much more suitable than others, but the overall quality was very high indeed—high enough to make my pulse race. I consumer-tested several dozen stones, right on the spot: ten skips, twelve skips, fourteen skips. And then I flung a stone that walked some eighty feet across the water, skipping more times than my astonished eyes could tally.

With a sudden pang, I thought about what fun I was having skipping stones out into Lake Champlain, but Lake Champlain was not within my kingdom. First, my hackles came up in envy; then, a few stones later, I felt myself lapsing into a deep funk. What cruel justice had placed this bounty so near to my lands and yet so far away? I retreated to the truck and sped home to nurse an oncoming migraine of regal angst.

Two weeks later, still bowed down with existential sorrow, something snapped inside me. I commanded my loyal kids to load the pickup with plastic five-gallon pails and to don their swimsuits. We were going to the state park to collect a haul of skipping-stones.

"I don't even know *how* to skip a stone," protested Ethan.

"That is just the point. Your life has been impoverished growing up around here. Now we're going to change all that."

"I don't even *care* about throwing rocks," Anaïs added.

"Just do as I say, for once," I begged them, striving hard to affect a royal air.

I timed our arrival at the state park for early evening, so we three could sneak out with several pails of skipping-stones under the cover of gathering dusk. My young subjects were no sooner out of the truck, though, when they found a sign posting various park rules and regulations. One of these—which they pointed out to me like cops—was that no one was allowed to disturb or remove any elements of the park's natural environment. "So, like what you're asking us to do is break the law," declared Ethan coolly.

"Just come on down to the water with me," I told him. "You'll see—God put a lifetime supply of stones here. I don't see how anyone is going to miss the few we need."

There was some grumbling, but no insubordination as we grabbed our pails and descended the steep, rocky trail to the shaley beach. Once we reached the water's edge, I had to educate my children about the ideal conformation of a skipping-stone; otherwise, they might have chosen imperfect rocks instead of the perfect ones that were there in abundance. Showing them how to choose wisely entailed teaching them how to actually skip a stone—and this course of instruction had consumed a good half hour before Ethan, in sheer frustration, went on strike and set off up the beach, fuming.

Anaïs, on the other hand, had progressed to the point where she could make every third stone bounce once before it sank. This level of minimal competency kept her in the game, but the last thing she wanted was to stop practicing and start collecting stones for our sneaky little heist. Very well; *I* set about collecting a pail of stones. There were several other people—campers, apparently—who had come down to the shingle to enjoy the approaching sunset, and one or two of these looked on my project with frank suspicion. Then the nagging voice of conscience started to assail me, giving words to their stern looks: *If everybody did this, before long there wouldn't be any stones here at all.* But a far more complicated urge began to work on me—the desire to immediately skip those really promising stones as soon as I found them. After all, why fight instant gratification?

I did fight it, though, and continued the patient work of filling my first pail even while my mind kept ruminating. I considered how, if I had a cache of A-1 skipping stones at our pond, this recreational ammo would soon become one more commodity I would perpetually run out of and have to replenish. Like hay, for example. Firewood. Diesel fuel. Baling twine. Grain. The fact was, much of my time as a farmer was devoted to stockpiling one or another of these items and then watching the stockpiles dwindle till they disappeared. King of the ranch or not, my life was ruled by recurring scarcities and the periodic need to replenish one stash or another. And would I now voluntarily add skipping-stones to my list?

In addition, having my own private supply of stones might make them hard to share. Could I gracefully stand by while visiting guests fired stone after stone from my pail out across the water? Would I have to implore them to go easy? Not to waste the good stuff? Would I, for that matter, have to ration my own pleasure in yet another recreational arena? Have to once again impose restraint, moderation, prudence? Would I have to remind myself, each time I skipped a stone, that now I possessed one fewer stone to skip?

There are occasional epiphanic moments in adult life, when a series of dimly recognized perceptions suddenly make perfect sense, showing one exactly where one stands. And what one stands for. I lifted up my pail—nearly three-quarters full—and its weight of gray rock tore the wire handle out of its notch in the plastic rim. Too many stones. It occurred to me that if I wanted to teach my children how to enjoy their lives, bringing them out here to take stones back to our place was a contradiction. Here were stones, and here was an excellent place to skip them. Next time we wanted to skip some stones, we could come back.

Up the beach, Ethan had taught himself to skip the odd stone roughly as well as his sister could; he prefers to learn things on his own. I called him back, and the three of us sent several hundred carefully selected, very nearly perfect stones hurtling into Lake Champlain in just a few minutes' time. Some of them skipped, some didn't, but the overall effect was like the finale to a well-paced fireworks show. A sudden, blazing surfeit. Far across the lake, the sun dipped behind the Adirondacks; when my pail was empty, we gathered up our belongings and left.

I still don't profess to know the secret to unending joy; I suspect there *is* no secret. But this abortive run for skipping-stones did mark a sea change in my attitude toward day-to-day happiness. The sort of kingship farming offers does require constant attention to provisioning; *living* like a king, though—it seems to me more and more—has little to do with acquiring and spending stores of one scarce commodity or another. Rather, it's a matter of enjoying moments thoroughly—of realizing even tiny pleasures to their hilt. Children, perhaps, do not need our help to learn such wisdom; for those lucky grown-ups who have not forgotten it, all the world's a private kingdom.

Learning to Work

A s a grown-up who was a child of the Sixties, I have tried to keep alive the dubious ideal that work ought to be *fun*, somehow. Just a grander form of play. And surely there are gratifying moments to be found in nearly every sort of labor. Starting new projects, for example, brings a certain joy. Also completing things. And all along the way come smaller, humbler satisfactions that derive from problems well solved and details well executed. I tremble to admit, however, that an awful lot of work turns out to be...well, *work*. There are certain attitudes that can help each person to endure his or her chosen labors, but insistence on a feeling of chronic euphoria simply isn't one of them. Learning how to grind things out can be far more useful.

For very young children, though, work and play often *do* seem to be identical. Whether the game is piling blocks, or shredding paper, or simply getting to one's feet and tottering across the room, its subject is the perfectly serious business of getting to know the world. How physical objects tend to cohere in time and space. How each material has its own unique set of physical properties. How sheer human will can alter some things but not others. Children tend to throw themselves into such creative work—er, play—with a concentration far deeper, and more focused, than we jaded adults are ever apt to muster. No surprise, then, that young children need more sleep than bricklayers or hairdressers. Or than surgeons, even.

Sooner or later, though, the time comes to acquaint the young with what adults regard as work. Sending kids off to school is one way that we try to do it, as though the job were too important for mere families to accomplish. On a farm, getting kids to tag along with grown-ups as they do their chores constitutes another way. At first children ask pointed questions and nod their heads. Later they may try their hand at whatever the task may be—mending fences, chopping wood, even shoveling manure. But all too soon, children tend to identify the Sisyphean character of most adult labors and wander off to find more sensible amusement.

And then, somehow, kids "grow up" and begin to see things our way. Whether this is wisdom or a sheeplike stupidity—mere flocking instinct—the fact is, *I* have known few greater pleasures than to watch my kids start handling grown-up work. Not because work holds any guarantees of ecstasy, but I would prefer a world of people who define themselves by things that they can do rather than by what they own or how they dress or where they travel. What's more—I was starting to feel kind of tired. I don't mind a little help.

Something else: it strikes me that our human lives are rather long. Time enough to try—and to succeed or fail—at many things. For those who come to learn its subtle, non-euphoric pleasures, working can fill many hours. Here, then, are some tales of watching children come to terms with work.

Matriculations

Nearly ten years ago, a Vermont neighbor was giving up the bucolic life and taking his family back to one of the great urban centers of the Northeast. Back to complicated living and to work that paid good money. He had a four-year-old son—as did I—and occasionally we would enjoy a sort of New Age coffee klatch of house-husbands whose wives were busy at their office jobs. Contemplating his upcoming move, my friend voiced concern over whether his son could get admitted to a top nursery school in the city that would be his home.

"What do you mean, get admitted?" I asked.

"You know—how they test kids nowadays?"

I did not know of it. "What do they have, baby S.A.T.s?"

"They have blocks and puzzles. Pictures. And they watch how well your kid can play. You know—with the other kids. How well socialized he is."

I shook my head. "Why bother?"

"Some of these nursery schools prepare kids for top kindergartens. Which feed them into certain grade schools. Which prep them for the prep schools, which—"

"I get it," I said. "Sort of cradle-to-grave."

"Huh?"

"I'll bet it all ends up in some Ivy League nursing home."

"You can laugh," he told me. "But I'm worried whether life in the sticks has prepared Jason all that well."

"For Nursery School Boards?"

"You don't seem to realize. A lot of four-year-olds can read, nowadays."

"*Mine* can't," I said. Proudly. "Ethan hasn't shown an interest, so I'm not encouraging him. He'll have lots of years ahead to read things, if that's what he wants."

"But—don't you care about your kid's intelligence?"

"Not a whole lot," I said. "If Ethan wants to turn out smart, that's *his* problem. I want him to turn out *nice*."

"Nice?"

"As in kind. Cheerful. Thoughtful of others. The world's chock full of smart people already. If smart people are going to save the planet, time is getting short."

"But—how are these kids going to make it without first-rate educations? They're going to be living in the twenty-first century."

"So am I, I hope," I told him.

"You think rural schools are going to teach Ethan the skills that he'll need?"

"I don't know. But I think they aren't likely to thwart him— which is half the battle. Or get in his way. Or channel him into something he might not have freely chosen."

"It's a question of creating opportunities."

"Okay." I shrugged, and we did not pursue the matter further. Parents can't help having aspirations for their children's futures, but I felt my friend expected just a bit too much of schooling. Then, too, I knew that school was where Ethan would first taste work—real, repetitive, uncreative, grown-up work. Phonics, spelling, multiplication tables...I wanted to watch him play for just a while longer.

In any event, my friend's young son passed muster for his urban nursery school. And then, in a stroke of colossal irony, Ethan's future public-school kindergarten summoned *him* to take what amounted to an admissions test—a "screening"—just a few months later. To see which of the kids in his class would be playing with a full deck, so to speak. And which ones would not. Remedial attention could then be lavished on the poorer child-scholars, prior to matriculation.

"Don't you worry," I told the school's secretary when she called to schedule an appointment. "My kid's going to ace this test."

She had been trained, however, to demur when eager parents made such bold and prejudicial statements. "We," she said, "shall see."

I did not subject my young son to a sudden crash course in blocks and vocabulary. Since Ethan seemed wonderfully alive intellectually and was a pleasant daily companion, I did not doubt that testers would recognize his talents. Even so, I recollect feeling a twinge of parental anxiety when the big morning came. Like a first trip to the dentist. We took a bath together, father and son; we combed our hair carefully and put on fresh, clean clothes. Best foot forward.

"What are they going to do to me?" he asked as we set off in the pickup truck.

"Just ask a bunch of questions, probably. It's no big deal."

"Questions about what?"

"Like, they may have a bunch of round pegs, okay? And a board with holes of different shapes. And the trick is not to put the round pegs in the square holes. Get it?"

He stared up at me, mystified.

"Just don't worry," I said.

At the ancient wooden schoolhouse, we sat in the corridor and filled out a bunch of forms while other kids were getting screened. The asphalt tiles in the hall smelled just like they had on *my* first day of school, thirty-three years before. The same brand of floor wax. My childhood started rushing before my eyes. Ethan, I realized, was climbing on a treadmill that would ultimately carry him away from me and into adulthood—into a life he would be free to define apart from our relationship, which seemed perfectly right and even necessary. But these things happen so fast. So quickly. Then, just as I was feeling poignant and a little sad, the testers called us in.

"You can watch," an efficient-looking woman told me. "But you aren't allowed to help him out, understand?"

"Yes, of course."

There were half a dozen workstations in the room, and the first involved matching geometric shapes in a series. Triangles with triangles, and so forth. It was no sweat. *My kid's going to score 100%*, I thought proudly. But the next station was a different story. Someone showed Ethan a series of drawings and asked him what he saw. First there was a horse.

My son squinted at the horse drawing for the longest time—until the tester repeated the question impatiently. "What is it you see?"

"I think—it looks almost just like a unicorn," Ethan replied. "Except that I don't see one single horn coming out of the middle of its forehead."

Does not recognize "horse," the tester wrote down on her card. Where, I had to wonder, had they turned up such a humorless battle-ax? Then I had a worse thought: looking at the woman critically, it struck me as all too plausible that she might be completely unfamiliar with unicorns. She stared at my son as at a moron, and asked pointedly: "Don't you see a *horse*?"

"I just don't think his ears are big enough. Do you?"

"*Horse.* That's a horse, there."

"Now, wait a second," I broke in. "Ethan and I play a game at home. We *study* pictures—*carefully*. We try to pick out if the artist made mistakes."

"Please," she said. "We can't allow you to offer advice."

"Horse," my son agreed lamely.

"Good. Now, try again—this picture." The tester flipped a card. "What is this girl doing?"

The drawing depicted a young girl in a bathtub, holding a washcloth poised a few inches in front of her face. My son studied this picture for a good twenty seconds.

"Well? What is she doing?"

"I don't know."

The woman started writing *Does not recognize Girl Washing Face*—writing, I must note, in a laborious and schoolmarmy cursive script that suggested the subordination of intellect to mere training. Halfway through, Ethan chirped up: "It looks almost as though she's trying to wash her face. Except—see? That cloth isn't touching her face at all. And I don't see any soap, either. Do you see soap?"

The tester put her pencil down and studied her test's drawing for the first time from the perspective of a sharp-eyed child. "No," she agreed. "I don't see soap."

"At *my* house, we wash with soap."

I could have hugged the kid. The tester carefully erased *Does not recognize*—and then she paused, completely stumped as to what to write down in its place. I had a few ideas: *Child finds mistake in test. Child recognizes that test sucks, big-time. Child sees more than tester.* After a moment's consideration, though, she decided to simply give him credit for the right answer.

Then came tests of auditory skills, fine motor skills—I've forgotten or repressed all the things they made him do. At the final station, Ethan had three chances to throw a volleyball into a round wastebasket several feet away. Here, I thought, they'll nail him: he'll get typed as bookish, academic, uncoordinated. My fault, too. I considered myself no slouch as a dad, but Ethan and I hadn't played catch since he was two years old.

I could see the ball felt huge and awkward in his childish hands; he was more surprised than I was, though, when he made a perfect free throw. Like he'd been in training. And again—three times, in fact.

"Hey!" I cried. "Now does he pass?"

"Kids don't pass or fail an evaluation like this," said the head tester.

Sure, I thought.

"But as for being ready for school—yes. He is."

I took a deep, proud breath. Of course, getting into my little town's public kindergarten is not the same as getting tracked for Harvard. Or any place else, for that matter. But education hasn't ruined my son, so far. He *does* want to grow up to be smart, the way things have turned out. Rural schools have taught him to read and write—and did not slow him down on account of awful penmanship. Moreover, they got him hooked on language; any given day, he reads and writes far more than I do. No one's tried to thwart him—or at least, no one's succeeded yet. Amazingly, schooling has made Ethan an authentic intellectual: he responds to experience in terms of ideas. That, I still maintain, may turn out to be his cross to bear—but could a tony private school in some upscale suburb hope to accomplish more?

In the meantime, my son is still nice to be around. And when he fails at something—anything, you just name it—my knee-jerk reaction is to think: *What kind of test was that?*

A Tree Walk

Winter surely cometh, and in her seventh autumn my daughter overheard me complain about the need to cut more firewood for our woodstoves. "You've already *got* a big pile of wood," Anaïs told me, aiming to console. "Downstairs, in the basement. Left over from last year."

I loaded a new file into its wooden holder and began sharpening my chainsaw's tired business end, tooth by battered tooth. "We do have a couple cords, but that won't see us through till spring—not unless we get off easy. Anyway, it's smart to try to get ourselves a year ahead. Cut wood now that we won't have to burn till *next* winter."

"Why?"

"So that it gets to season."

"What does *season* mean?"

I took a deep breath, thinking how best to explain this concept to her. "When you cut a tree down, a lot of what's inside is water. Gallons and gallons of water, tucked away inside a zillion little cells. People call that *green* wood, and it takes a lot of drying out before the wood burns really well. Some trees—like red oak or maple—may take one whole year to dry. Sometimes you'll get green logs burning, but you're boiling so much water that the fire can't get hot, because—do you really want to hear this?"

"Sure," she said, sounding not the least bit sure. She did seem intent, though, on my fiddling with the saw. It is a frightening and rapacious sort of tool. She knew it; I knew it.

"Much of the *potential* heat in firewood comes as gases, which are volatile—just vapors, see? But many of those gases only burn at high temperatures. The moisture in unseasoned wood keeps a fire too cool to get those fumes ignited. So instead, they go right up the chimney—unburned. Wasted."

"Is that like pollution?"

"Maybe. Sure—I guess it is. But mainly, if we burn green wood, we lose part of its heat. Understand?"

She nodded, doing her best to keep the old man humored. I could tell she didn't want to know that much about it.

"Anyway, once firewood is all dried out, we call it *seasoned.* You can tell—it weighs much less, and at the end of every log are little cracks from shrinkage. Then you get a good, hot fire. So we need to cut wood *now* to let it season for next winter."

"How many trees do you chop down, to get a whole year's wood?"

I suppose I might have told her *Quite a few* or even *Dozens.* But I was just settling into my Explanatory Mode, which can be a cunning means to procrastinate when some all-too-aerobic chore like lumberjacking waits. So I said, "It all depends."

Anaïs pulled a face. "On what?"

"On the size of trees you cut, and on what kind of trees, and the shape of—listen, how about this idea? You and I could cruise the woods and pick out next winter's trees. And then I'll just notch them quickly with the saw, so—"

"I don't like the sound of the chainsaw," she informed me tersely.

"We don't have to notch them, then. We could leave the saw right here." Fact is, I was only too happy to find a way to postpone real forest work for yet another day. "But we need *some* way to mark our trees. So when I go back in a couple days to cut them down, I'll only drop the ones we picked. What do you think—maybe we could give them paint marks?"

Now it was her turn to be as difficult as I can be. "I think if it started raining hard, the paint might wash right off."

"Well, then how about tying lengths of ribbon around each trunk? Don't you have some ribbon somewhere?"

"I just have some bows, except I'm saving them. For wrapping presents. It's going to be Christmas, soon."

"What, then?"

I watched her mental wheels spin, and then she went to ransack a closet where the kids store crayons and drawing paper and offbeat art supplies. She returned carrying a recycled grocery bag filled with cardboard cores from old toilet-paper rolls. Dozens and dozens of them. Half a year's worth.

"What have you been saving *these* for?"

"Ethan and I use them for projects sometimes. Making things."

"Such as?"

"Animals, or dolls, or—or a lot of things. You can use these, though. There's more."

"Well, we're going to need some way to fasten them to tree trunks."

"Maybe thumbtacks?"

"Thumbtacks," I agreed. "Why not? You go find some thumbtacks, then put on long pants. We're going to the woods."

Twenty minutes later we were tramping through the woodlot, sizing up tree after tree, poised to mark candidates for felling with this crazy badge. I carried the bag of toilet-paper cores, and Anaïs carried a Tupperware bowl of brightly colored pushpins. It was the thirteenth year of my commitment to home-grown firewood as our source of winter heat, and the forest vistas had begun to change considerably. The tree population, once far too thick and crowded, had become very palpably thinned. Old stumps poked up everywhere—waiting to be tripped over—and great piles of twigs and branches too small to deal with lay gradually rotting into the forest floor. And it was quite clear, this autumn, that all the really appropriate firewood had long since been taken.

"How about that one there?" Anaïs asked, pointing to an ancient sugar maple in the middle distance.

"Way too big. I'd have to split each chunk six or seven times."

"Well, that?" She chose a slender hardhack.

"That's a good *kind* of tree, but that one's not quite big enough."

"Maybe over there?"

"Nice size and shape, but that's a linden tree. Or basswood, as Vermonters call it."

"So?"

"Honey, we might as well burn newspapers as basswood. There's just not much heat in a tree like that. Know why?"

"No. Why?"

"It has to do with density—now wait, just listen. *Density* means what an object weighs for its size. Do you understand about hardwoods and softwoods?"

"No."

"That might be just as well. Both those words can be misnomers."

"What does *that* mean?"

"Not a good name. When a name is too confusing."

"You've got *me* confused," she echoed.

"Okay—softwoods are your pine trees, more or less. Your conifers—trees that carry needles on their branches instead of leaves. And cones, too. Compared to oaks or beeches or maple trees, the wood in a conifer isn't nearly as dense. But *hardwood* just refers to trees that—well, to keep it simple, trees with *leaves* instead of needles. It doesn't go based on hardness at all, really. Because some trees, like that basswood, get classified as hardwoods when they aren't even as dense as pine. Basswood weighs about twenty-five pounds per cubic foot, but the same piece of oak weighs *twice* as much. So—well, like I said. There's not enough heat in basswood to be worth our trouble."

But she was walking away from me now, bored with this arcana. I couldn't blame her. She was certainly getting the hang of identification, though: pointing to another tree, she asked me, "Basswood?"

"Right."

And then another: "Basswood?"

"Yes."

"How come we have so many basswood trees?"

"Because—well, I guess because I never cut them down. Because basswood makes such terrible firewood."

"Aren't they good for anything?"

"Sure," I told her. "Shaker boxes. Like that nesting set of oval boxes at your Grandma's."

"Maybe you should start making Shaker boxes, then."

"Maybe I will—someday. Meantime, let's just say we're saving up our basswoods." To myself, I thought: *I have been "saving up" these basswoods for years. Many have grown past their prime. And chances are they'll all be right here—worthless—after I am gone.*

Anaïs was also putting two and two together; she broke into my dismal train of thought to tell me, "After a while, then, all you're going to *have* is basswoods. If you never chop them down."

"I'm afraid so, honey—basswoods, and all the other trees I think have something wrong with them." I had to hand it to her: she had put her finger on the cardinal sin in my considerably short-sighted, need-driven practice of forest management. I treat the woodlot like a garden in which only vegetables get picked, and never a single weed. Run things this way long enough, and undesired species—weed trees—are just bound to take control. I said, "There is always more work in this woodlot than I seem to get around to."

"*That* tree's not a basswood," she said, pointing.

"No. That one's an elm."

"It looks pretty dead, too—is it?"

"Nearly all the elms are dead now. Everywhere. On account of the Dutch Elm Disease."

"So you could chop down that one, couldn't you?" Anaïs had

picked out a blue-tipped tack, and now she reached into the bag of toilet-paper cores.

"Not so fast," I told her. "I don't like to mess with elms."

"Why not?"

"Elm is hard to split. The grain spirals through the trunk, and splitting wedges just get stuck. I think life is far too short."

"It is?"

"That's just an expression. It means—"

"What do we do with elms, then?"

"After a while they fall down, and then we let them rot."

"*There's* a different kind of tree," she said. "What kind is that?"

"White ash. You know what they use white ash for?"

"No."

"All kinds of sports equipment. Baseball bats, hockey sticks—"

"Why?"

"The wood has long, straight fibers that make it really strong. Makes it easy to split, too—one good whack will do it. Right down the middle."

"Does it make good firewood?"

"Excellent firewood. And you know what? Even when it's green, ash gives a lot of heat."

She went to feel the smooth, silver-gray bark. "Want me to tack a toilet-paper roll on it?"

"Maybe. Here's what you and I had better decide, though: see how tall and straight that trunk is? That's a really *good* ash tree. Primo. That tree could probably get cut up in a sawmill, someday—for a fair amount of money. That tree could be made into an awful lot of hockey sticks. So the thing is, should we cut it down to help us heat our house, or should we let it grow up into something much more valuable?"

I watched Anaïs ponder this Godlike decision. Then she asked: "*How* valuable?"

"Eight or ten dollars at the roadside. Of course, we would have to drag it out there with the tractor. And we'd need to cut *enough* ash trees to fill a log truck, and then sell them all at once."

"Is ten dollars very much money?"

"Sure, I guess—for one ash tree."

"Have you *got* a whole truckload?"

"Not yet. Say, in twenty years."

I was not surprised to see she couldn't grasp time on this scale; looking around the forest, I had manifestly failed to take the long view, myself. "Dad," she said, "you've got to chop down *some*thing if you want to get firewood. Every tree I ask about, you—"

"Right. My sentiments exactly." I handed her a cardboard toilet-paper core and watched her affix it gently to the ash's trunk. "After all, firewood *does* have a cash value. Maybe not too much, but that's the only way this forest ever seems to make us money."

"How much money does it make us?"

"Actually, none—but if we had to buy a whole year's wood, we'd pay several hundred dollars. And if we had oil heat, we'd spend a lot more. So the forest is like money your Mom and I don't have to earn."

"There's another ash tree, over there. You think?"

"Sure. Go claim it."

She ran off to mark her victim, then stopped short as though realizing, for the first time, what it was that we were doing. "Dad?"she asked me. "You know a lot about trees, don't you?"

"Yes," I said. "A fair amount. Just from cutting firewood."

"Do you think these trees are living?"

"Yes, of course—but not like people. Not like animals, or—"

"What's so different?"

"Trees don't talk, or think. Trees don't hurt—they don't have feelings."

"Are you sure?"

"Well, of course I can't be sure. I've even read of tribes where people say a prayer to trees before they cut them down."

"What kind of prayer is that?"

"Sort of to apologize. Sort of to give thanks."

"Do you do that?"

"No, I never have. I'm always too busy thinking where the tree should drop. The safest path. The best direction. Felling trees is dangerous work, you know?"

"Yes. I know that." She turned around again to tack the toilet-paper core onto the ash she'd chosen. "Sorry," I heard her tell the tree. "But thanks a lot. You can keep us nice and warm next winter."

Which, I thought, *was* taking a pretty long view, especially for a seven-year-old. "Good work," I told Anaïs.

"Dad? I'm getting tired of this. I'm going back to the house."

"Sure, honey. Fine." I watched her tiptoe from the woods, then cruised the forest on my own to note more trees just waiting to be sacrificed. To become our fuel. I spared them Anaïs' toilet-paper badge of honor, but I memorized their approximate locations. And, in my own way, I apologized and thanked them, too: much wood has been harvested, but we have many trees to go. I found little cause to fear the coming nights of bitter cold—not just yet, at least. And when I thought hard about it, I found little cause to fear the coming cold at all.

Night Riders

Most of the hundred-odd lambs our sheep bring forth each spring grow big enough to be chauffeured to market in early autumn. By then, I am glad to start hauling them off the farm before they can eat me into serious financial trouble. In the final, "finishing" stages of producing lamb chops—when each animal is laying down the white fat that our culture has come to simultaneously prize and fear—a typical lamb will guzzle thirty cents' worth of grain per day, converting it into maybe half a dollar's worth of meat. Because the feed company demands payment for its grain long before we start receiving proceeds from the fattened lambs, cash flow can become horrendous. Running such a business out of the family checkbook, it's not hard to get embarrassingly stretched.

Then, along about November, things get back in balance; by the time snow starts to fly, I expect to calculate some modest profits. Still, there may be half a dozen critters not yet off the chow line. "Poor-doers," shepherds call them—lambs who maybe grew up stunted, or got sick at one point, or just lacked the genes for growth rate and carcass size and feed conversion that drove their compatriots to make faster, thriftier, less expensive gains. The sad news is that an unabashed poor-doer can eat *half a dollar's worth* of feed to achieve a daily gain worth no more than a quarter. Such lambs are hard to love. But we go on feeding them anyway, because the marketing co-operative to which we sell our animals has little use for lambs that won't "dress out" at more than forty-five pounds.

Most years, we get the poor-doers off the farm along about Thanksgiving; some years we wind up feeding them till Christmas. And in the worst case—such as just a couple years ago—we may have those last few lambs on our hands past New Year's. This gets unamusing, because marketing our lambs requires loading them onto the pickup and driving them ninety miles to Jeff Nichols Slaughterhouse in South Barre, Vermont. In the teeth of winter, it's a tough haul. And the lambs need to arrive around six-thirty in the morning because the kill line starts up at the dot of seven. Allowing time to brew a pot of coffee, load the truck, and then negotiate a couple hours of icy highways, there's no way to be on time without leaving bed at three.

Even before entering his teenage years, Ethan had begun to keep the erratic hours associated with adolescence. He has many projects; there are seldom enough hours in his busy days. Still, I was surprised to tiptoe down the hall in the wee hours of a January morning and find my son sitting in the study, bathed in the computer monitor's amber glow and banging away on the keyboard, processing words. "What are *you* doing up?" I whispered.

"Working on a book."

"At quarter past three?"

"I couldn't sleep."

"So what's this book about?"

"King Arthur. Sorry—did I wake you?"

"No." I pulled the curtains back and peered out the window. Snow was moving sideways past the glass, but I couldn't tell if it was a fresh storm or just the old stuff getting blown into new drifts. "I'm driving our last lambs to the slaughterhouse—you want to ride shotgun?"

"What does that mean?"

"Help me stay awake. Tell stories. Sing songs."

"I have school, you know?"

"I think I can drop you off in time, on the way back."

He thought it over, then said yes. I went to brew the coffee, charging him to dress in layers just as though we were going downhill skiing. It was two degrees out, but the truck started painlessly and I let it warm up in the driveway till the heater worked. Then we piled in and slalomed down to the barn, crunching through old snow with a thin veneer of softer, more powdery flakes on top.

"How are you going to get those lambs onto the truck?" asked Ethan.

"Easy. They've been chugging grain, and that has made them starved for hay. I'll back up against the loading dock and work the gate, while you go get a bale of hay and break it open on the truck-bed. Show them what you're doing, and those lambs should file right in. Works like a charm."

But it wasn't a charmed morning—not with the wind kicking up in bitter gusts, not with packed snow pasted all across the steel truck-bed. Those last seven lambs backed off and stared at me as if to say: "You're crazy. Would *you* leave a cozy barn to climb aboard that rig?"

I tried coaxing them with grain, but they had seen enough of that. Salt, too. Finally I called Ethan up onto the barn floor with me, and we lashed wooden pallets together with baling twine to fashion a funnel-shaped chute. It took twenty precious minutes to construct, and we found we could not tie the knots while wearing heavy gloves. Our fingers reddened, then turned numb before we had the whole thing built. Once we drove the first lamb out onto the pickup, though, his half-dozen buddies gave in and quickly followed.

It was after four when I slammed the tailgate shut and joined Ethan in the cab. "You can change your mind," I told him. "You have helped me out, already."

"No. Come on, let's go."

I put the truck in low-range and crabbed sideways, scrambling to get up onto the crown of the driveway. It was snowing briskly now, and windblown snow had totally filled in the drive's front slope, down by the mailbox where I had carefully plowed just the day before. Then, gearing up as we swung onto the paved road, the truck's rear end fishtailed on glare ice.

"This could be a hairy run," I predicted just as we felt the lambs stagger across the truck-bed, seeking their own traction.

"Maybe you should have hauled those lambs right after supper."

"Maybe. But I hate to make them spend the whole night up there, waiting."

"You ready for some coffee?"

I nodded. "You will have to hold my cup, though. This is two-handed driving."

We crawled along for twenty miles at a speed so cautious it seemed we might never get to South Barre. At times, snow whipped across the road with such intensity that I had to judge the shoulder's edge from memory. Ethan held a steaming mug up to my lips with one hand, searching the radio bands with the other to find a weather update. Few Vermont stations, though, stay on the air all night; first he pulled in Albany, then Buffalo and Cincinnati. And then he managed to turn up Chicago, albeit with a lot of static. "Wow!" he crowed. "Chicago is a thousand miles away! Their weather won't help us, though."

"Actually, it might," I countered. "I don't think we'd *get* those stations if this were a real storm. Just a little squall, I'll bet. It takes a cold, clear night to pull Chicago in."

Sure enough, by Shelburne the snow had started tapering. And then, south of Burlington, we rolled out of the clouds altogether. A frigid moon was setting to the west, above the Adirondacks; overhead a billion stars were pinning back the night. It was more than beautiful, and beneath our wheels the pavement now turned clear and dry. Every tribulation, I thought, ought at times to stand revealed as similarly local. Circumscribed. Minuscule. The radio station started booming in effortlessly, and I doubted there could be one cloud between us and Chicago.

"I could write a poem about those stars," Ethan announced.

" 'Hauling Lambs in Winter,' " I said. " 'Underneath the Sky.' "

"Sure."

We hit the empty interstate and drove along in silence, keeping at a steady sixty miles per hour. Barring new surprises, we would get our lambs to South Barre in the nick of time. "When you were three or four years old," I recalled for Ethan, "you drove with me to slaughterhouses all over New England. Manchester, Boston, Hartford—you remember those trips?"

"No."

"That was before we had a marketing co-operative."

"Now do you always just drive to South Barre?"

"For the last few years. We used to go to Hyde Park, till they said they wanted eight dollars there to kill a lamb."

"How much does South Barre charge?"

"Only seven-fifty, and the co-op gets to keep the pelts. But the best thing is, at this place lambs go right into the building. They just hop down off the truck, because the holding pen at Nichols's looks like someone's barn. It looks *friendly* and—well, I guess *inviting*. Some of these brand-new, concrete-and-steel kill plants, it takes an electric stock-prod to get lambs in the door."

"That's cruel."

"I guess it is. Anyway, the place we're using now is real nice. Humane. I've never seen our lambs get scared there."

"How can *you* tell?"

"When they all bunch up and sort of freeze? That tells me they're afraid."

"Maybe they *should* be afraid. Aren't they going to die?"

"They are going to die, but they can still be treated gently. They can still be treated with respect. They don't have to die in a state of fear, or terrorized, or—"

"Okay, Dad. I get it." But I watched him consider these thoughts for another several miles. Then he yawned a great yawn and laid his head across my lap. He said: "I am going to sleep now."

First light was just breaking, forty minutes later, when I backed the pickup into the unloading chute at Nichols's. I managed to creep from the truck's cab without waking Ethan, then dropped the tailgate and climbed up into the bed. "Hwisst! Hwisst!" I urged, clapping my hands a couple times, and the year's last lambs jumped off the truck to join some fifty-odd others who stood waiting, calm and patient, in the freshly bedded holding pen. It was five minutes to seven.

I pulled down a clipboard hanging from a rusty nail and entered my name and the numbers on the ear tags we had given each lamb at birth. Now the only lambs I owned lay deep inside their mothers' wombs, waiting to be born in April. Thinking ahead to them, I climbed behind the wheel again and drove a sleeping helper out into the dawn.

Driving Lesson

In an earlier, less-harried age, farm families specialized in raising children by the dozen. Each new mouth to feed meant two more hands to help with chores; all things considered, this was not a bad bargain. Today's farms, however—at least those here in New England—are predicated on having not piles of children but tons of cold steel. Machinery. One person at the controls of a modern tractor can do the work of an army of ragamuffins. Tractors are expensive, true, but so are tuitions when one's ragamuffins grow up and decide they want to

go to college.

Mindful of these trade-offs, Cheryl and I stopped our procreative efforts after the birth of our second child. This was a decade ago, and sometimes it feels like we've been waiting ever since for those kids to start spelling us at farm work. For years they were just too young, of course, to operate machinery, and the sort of chores that we still perform by hand—feeding and watering, trimming hoofs, rotating pastures—seemed understandably prosaic to a child's mind. Or to an intelligent grown-up's, for that matter.

Even the big-time chores, like driving a tractor, are not nearly so exciting and creative as they first appear. Oh, it feels good to mount a brutish, complicated steed. Making fifty horsepower spring to whining life with the flick of a key can seem a compelling confirmation of a person's prowess. Once one starts to mow a given field, though—or to rake it, bale it, fertilize it, plow it, smooth it, seed it—one very quickly finds oneself going around in circles. Hour after hour after mind-numbing hour. A certain level of skill with the controls is required, of course, as well as an unflagging alertness for potential trouble. But creative mental processes shut down altogether, and "farming" soon becomes just one more exercise in time and distance.

I don't spend a whole lot of time riding a tractor—no more than a couple hundred hours in an average year—but by the time Ethan turned thirteen, I had begun sizing him up as potential relief driver. His legs were finally long enough to reach the pedals and strong enough to tromp on the clutch and hold it disengaged. He had become capable of sustained concentration, and competent to exercise sound judgment in a pinch. Furthermore, he had reached the age where mastering machinery starts to become a complicated metaphor for emerging manhood. Why deny him? So, one midsummer morning, I announced that it was time for us to start his tractor-driving lessons.

He took the news with surprising equanimity. "Do I need to wear shoes?" he asked.

"Absolutely."

"Then I'll have to find them."

"Find a hat, too, while you're at it. With a broad visor." Never too soon to start protecting against skin cancer.

While he went to sack his bedroom, I considered that he'd also need to protect his ears. I planned to take him out to mow an overgrown, weedy pasture, and our mowing machine is a high-decibel implement. Many lifelong farmers are as deaf as aging rock stars, but I was determined not to start my young son down that road to silence. "Put on these, too," I told him when he came back shod. "These are hearing protectors."

He fingered my industrial-grade earmuffs, then returned them to me. "Those are yours, Dad."

"So? I'm going to let you use them."

"What are *you* going to wear?"

"I'll just do without, for once."

"No. I'll get my earwax."

I nodded at the sensibility of this proposal. Evenings on our farm are ordinarily tranquil, but at weaning time we have one hundred lambs bawling to their mothers all night long. None of us would sleep a wink without the aid of earwax. Since we had just recently been through the din of weaning, he still had two pink blobs sitting on the shelf beside his bed.

Moments later, properly armed and equipped, we walked out to approach the tractor. I felt grateful for having decided, several years before, to trade up to a new machine with many built-in safety features. Our tractor won't start, for example, if it has been left in gear or has a power-take-off implement poised to start its whirling business. I motioned Ethan to sit on the fender while I showed him the various interlocks that had to be disarmed before the engine would turn over; then I started up the diesel.

Then I turned it off. "Your turn."

He slid behind the wheel. Trying out the clutch, he had to perch on the edge of the driver's seat and brace himself to push the pedal to the floor. "Won't this seat adjust?" he asked me.

"Wait. I'll check the manual."

Boy, did it adjust. There was a meter on the seat back where we dialed in his weight—in kilos—to change the spring tension, and a steel plate that let the seat slide down and forward until a midget could have worked the pedals. Once we got that right, he brought the engine back to life.

"Okay," I began. "Now, there are two basic safety rules for—"

"What?"

"*Safety.* If you—"

"*What??* "

I recognized the cause of our communication problem. He had his hearing protection and I had mine, and with the tractor's motor running, we could scarcely hear each other. So we disarmed our ears while I continued with my little safety lecture.

"There are two main ways that people maim or kill themselves on tractors. First, they roll it over on a sidehill and crush themselves. Second, they mow themselves or bale themselves or otherwise get worked over by a moving implement."

Ethan's eyes widened, and he looked prepared to climb right off.

"Neither of these accidents ever has to happen to you," I continued. "When you're on a sidehill, *think.* Slow down. Give yourself some leeway. Even if you lose it, though, this tractor has a built-in roll bar. And it's got a seat belt, too—*use* it, and you can't get crushed."

I watched Ethan buckle up.

"Second, never *ever* leave the tractor seat before the implement you're running has come to a stop—*completely.* Sometimes that takes fifteen seconds, sometimes a minute. But if you just sit right here waiting, you can't get chewed up. Understand?"

He nodded soberly. "Dad—just in case I need to, how do I turn this thing off?"

I pointed to the kill-switch on the dash, a bright orange knob marked STOP. "Pulling that out shuts the fuel off. Stops the engine quick. You want to try it?"

"No—I believe you."

"Okay. Let's go mow a field."

I helped him choose a gear whose speed he could control with relative ease, and soon we were going round and round a scruffy pasture, knocking down rank grass and thick, ambitious burdocks. Ethan's pattern was nowhere near perfect—there were missed streaks of grass between several of his swaths, and several ragged corners where he overshot on turns—but in a couple hours he got the mower to behave predictably. Doing such field work is much harder than driving a tractor down the road; the operator has to keep attention divided between front-end steering choices and whatever the implement is doing, ten or fifteen feet behind. Any slight adjustment of one's course at the steering wheel takes several moments to affect the mower's attitude, so one has to plan one's route well in advance.

For my part—once I felt convinced we weren't about to crash and burn—I started seeing things I seldom notice when I'm at the wheel. Red-tailed hawks circling high above us in the sky and barn swallows flying aerobatics over new-mown swaths, skimming off a meal. I even spied a fox dancing at the forest's edge. After a while I felt vague stirrings of alarm and realized the reason. "There's a half-buried rock around here some-where," I shouted to my young driver. "Keep your eyes peeled, so you can steer the mower around it."

"How do you know there's a rock?"

"Because I have hit it. Right *there*—see?"

He saw the rock and expertly skirted the machine around it, and I thought: *He's going to learn these fields just as well as I have. Every contour, each last wrinkle. Like the back of his own hand.*

Soon enough, Ethan had mowed his first three acres. He disen-gaged the implement and aimed us back toward the barn. When we got there, I told him to pull up by the grain bin—and he tried to by pulling out the STOP knob. The engine died, predictably, but still we kept rolling forward.

"Brakes!" I hollered.

"Where are they?"

I lurched off the fender and slammed one foot onto the brakes a moment before the wooden bin would have become trash. We stopped in the nick of time, then eyed each other nervously.

"I killed the motor, like you said!"

"But the wheels have brakes, of course. You have to use the brakes, if—"

"Dad, you didn't tell me!"

"Sorry—I forgot. Well—now I guess you know about them."

He tried the brakes out—two separate pedals, one for each rear drive-wheel.

I said, "On the whole, you did pretty darn good. Ethan—do you *like* driving?"

He nodded gamely. "I will get the hang of this."

Having a dozen kids to raise here, as in the good old days, might be awfully amusing; being the father of the right two, though, is quite enough. Any day now, I expect to hand over my tractor key.

Lambing with Kids

My career as a Vermont shepherd has roughly coincided with my career as a parent; fourteen years ago my young wife, Cheryl, and our brand-new flock of ewes both brought forth their firstborn. Watching ovine life helped me to trust the latent parenting instincts that I found I harbored. As these managed to assert themselves, I also gained confidence in our ewes' ability to supervise the care and nurture of their bleating offspring. Adventures in the lambing barn thus served to inform adventures in the nursery, and vice versa. It seemed a perfect two-way street.

Infants have a knack for turning into kids, however, which can unbalance such pretty equations. Ethan was barely four years old when he first boldly challenged my competence at shepherding. The circumstance involved the sort of lamb one brings into the house at scarcely two days of age: gaunt, hypothermic, and much too weak to suckle. Several fairly common scenarios produce such cases—poor maternal bonding, or a blocked teat canal, or a lamb with sharp teeth—and half a dozen common tricks can usually resuscitate such chilled and hungry customers. First, I pushed a catheter tube into this patient's stomach and force-fed it a cup of milk; then I wrapped the lamb in a warm towel and gave it a brisk massage; then, with its body stretched supine on the brick hearth by our woodstove, I injected dextrose into each of the lamb's four armpits. Nothing seemed to work, though, so—with hope now fading fast—I moved on to the high-risk whisky cure, forcing a nip of hard stuff down the lamb's throat. Gasoline, so to speak. But the lamb was too far gone to exhibit much surprise at being thus made to belly up to the bar. Ten minutes later, it was virtually comatose.

At first my son had helped me with these efforts at revival, but as each new stunt proved of limited avail he carefully distanced himself from my ministrations. Ethan kept watching in wide-eyed astonishment, gradually but palpably losing faith in my supposed expertise at caring for the livestock on which I had founded my agrarian identity. Finally, as the ill-fated lamb's chest was heaving out its last few breaths, my four-year-old asked pointedly: "Daddy—are you *sure* you know what you're doing?"

"Look, we did our best," I told him. "But for some reason this lamb couldn't make it."

"Now it's dead, right?"

"I'm afraid so." I studied Ethan's disappointed face, then thought of an ambitious strategy for regaining his confidence. I asked him: "Want to find out why?"

"How can we do that?"

I carried the corpse out onto the back porch, then stropped a skinning knife to keen its gleaming blade. The most common cause of death in very young lambs is simple starvation, and it scarcely takes a minute to confirm such a diagnosis with a quick post-mortem. I zipped the lamb's belly open to examine stomach contents: here was my milk-feeding, there was my shot of booze, and elsewhere were quantities of yellow-white, cottage-cheesy goop—partially digested mother's milk—indicating that the lamb had been adequately nourished.

Ruling out starvation, I moved on to check the lungs and found two healthy, bright-pink sponges without any trace of pneumonic distress. Finally I checked the lamb's tail for signs of acute diarrhea—"scours"—which can knock out day-old lambs by virtual dehydration. But the entire anal region was clean. Having ruled out all three leading causes of mortality, I felt frankly stumped. And a trifle embarrassed, too.

"Well?" Ethan asked, having for the first time seen what makes a lamb tick...or what is *supposed* to. The ultimate pocket watch—except that, once disassembled, there is no way it can be made to run again.

"I don't know," I told him. "I can't figure this one out."

When a very young lamb dies, shepherds seldom deem it a total loss; the skin can be peeled off and draped over some hungry triplet to trick a grieving mother into faith in resurrection. Ethan watched, fascinated, as I performed this miracle. When the dead lamb's mother had agreed to love a strange baby who arrived dressed in her lost kid's birthday suit, I felt sure that a measure of paternal respect had been restored to my son's bright, ingenuous eyes. Still there was the matter of why an apparently healthy lamb had failed to thrive, and the plain fact was that I didn't have a clue. Furthermore, next time I attempted to engage Ethan in the simplest barnyard chores, he refused politely but quite firmly. Who, I thought, could blame him?

Not long after, Ethan's sister came into the world; Anaïs fell in love with sheep, I think, even before she had learned to crawl. As our flock of breeding ewes swelled to over eighty, I got the bright idea to build a heated office in the barn—suspended from the rafters, with a glass observation wall that overlooked the flock—so that we could better supervise lambing chores which now stretched on for several weeks at a time. The barn office was tiny, but it held a desk, an overstuffed chair, and a narrow mattress; one could get a reasonably good night's sleep up there even at the peak of lambing, peering out occasionally to scan the floor below for labor activity. Best of all, the office made it possible for me to spend time with my kids—*quality* time, I liked to imagine—during an otherwise hectic and exhausting season.

Staying overnight in the barn office was an instant hit with both children—sort of like going on a wonderful camping trip without really leaving home. Since the bed was small—and since I deemed the office's electric heater a potential danger—the ground rules were that only one kid could come out each night and that a grown-up had to be there. Ethan, on his barn nights, proved utterly oblivious to whatever bleating dramas were unfolding right beneath us; he would study books, make games, and swap lies with me till his eyes closed involuntarily. Anaïs, on the other hand, relished any chance to descend from the barn office and check matters on the floor. In time, I found a job for her that proved completely helpful: checking the temperatures of very young lambs to make certain that they were metabolizing energy.

When fever is no issue, a lamb's temperature is checked merely by sticking a finger deep into its mouth. The mouth should feel *hot*; in the first few days of life, though, a lamb's internal thermostat can go abruptly on the blink. Lukewarm mouths tend to bear careful watching, and a cold

mouth requires immediate attention. Cold mouths, too, are usually accompanied by sagging flanks and rigid postures—symptoms of an empty stomach. Noticed while still on their feet, such lambs aren't hard to save; having a child who would willingly lose sleep to check each young mouth in the barn proved beneficial, over the years, to many lambs who were flirting with catastrophe.

Anaïs was four or five—just about the age when I had stunted her brother's budding interest in the nuts and bolts of shepherding—when she reported a cold-mouthed lamb who *didn't* appear to be hungry. I went with her to have a look. Sure enough, the lamb was apparently well fed, but it stood with its back humped, wobbling on uncertain legs without the slightest interest in suckling his mom's ripe breast. "I don't get it," I told Anaïs sleepily.

"Doesn't it look just like she's trying to poop?"

I considered correcting this child vernacular with better vocabulary, but it seemed a futile project. Anaïs had a point, though: the lamb now winced, half squatting on its haunches with tail stretched out erect. Just as though it were straining to move its bowels. I had never heard of such a thing before, but I had to agree with my daughter. I said: "That lamb looks awfully constipated."

"So what can we do?"

Shepherds are allowed to bother each other with phone calls seeking emergency advice, and it wasn't too late to call a woman in a nearby town who had raised far more lambs in her career than I had. "Sure," this colleague told me. "Sounds just like a lamb who hasn't passed its fetal dung. Colostrum-milk is a laxative, but it doesn't always work. That lamb's all plugged up, and it won't feel like eating till there's someplace for the milk to go."

"Is there any cure?"

"Try giving it an enema."

"The hell?" I asked, astounded. "How?"

"Take an old plastic syringe without a needle and squirt a bit of soapy water up past the anus. Then stand back—in five minutes, your lamb should be on the mend."

Back in the barn, I explained to Anaïs what we had to do; she watched, unflappable, as we pumped warm lubricant into the surprised lamb's bowel. Out snaked a long, dark package of tar. Half an hour later, the much relieved baby was happily suckling her mother's soft, bulging udder. "Gee," I told Anaïs. "I think I've just figured out why an important lamb died here, several years ago."

"Oh?" She yawned sleepily.

"Absolutely. In the morning, let's tell Ethan all about this."

Ethan was not mightily impressed with my tardy diagnosis. Checking for signs of constipation, though, was added to our routine observation of newborns; in consequence, over the past few years we've saved another several lambs who might otherwise have died and been chalked up to mystery hypothermia. Meanwhile, the kids have continued growing up—Ethan is a teenager now and no longer shy with sheep, and Anaïs recently turned nine. Their interest in the life of our flock has flowered even as my own enthusiasm has started to wane. Just this past spring, the day came when I felt sick and tired of lambing chores—when I wanted to do nothing more, one Saturday night, than to put on clean clothes and take Cheryl out dancing. But it had been raining lambs for much of that afternoon, and the barn was full of newborns needing to be squared away.

"Sure—you guys go out," said Ethan. "Anaïs and I can sleep out in the barn."

"That's against the rules," I told him. "Only one child per night, and there has to be a grown-up."

"We can do it," said Anaïs. "We're not babies anymore. Go on, have some fun. Just trust us."

"Can we let them do this?" I asked Cheryl. "All by themselves?"

"If they're sure they want to." My wife shrugged, no longer young herself and looking, all at once, like an incipient empty-nester. So we watched, with moist eyes, as our little ones packed their p.j.'s, toothbrushes, art supplies, and midnight snacks and set out together to supervise the lambing barn. I don't imagine any distant, future rite of passage—gaining driver's licenses, graduating, getting married—is apt to make so startling an impression on us. Then we washed up, put on our dancing shoes, and stepped out to enjoy the night.

When we got home—late—I dropped by the barn to see how things were going for the kids. Both of them were still awake, up in the office, and they came right out when they saw me checking pens.

"Dad," said Ethan, "you've got trouble."

"Where?"

"Here, let me show you."

He came down, followed by his sister, and they led me to a pen where a young triplet stood exhibiting the classic signs of newborn constipation. Anaïs pointed: "That one—see?"

"Well, I know just what to do here. Don't you kids remember?"

"Dad—"

"You fill an old syringe with warm, soapy water, push it past the anus and—"

"Dad, he hasn't *got* an anus!"

"Oh, come on."

"Go ahead—just look."

I picked up the lamb and lifted its tail, and—surprise, surprise. Dumbstruck, I carried him over to a lightbulb's glare and took a closer look. Absolutely nothing there. Smooth as a cheek, extending my understanding of anal-retentive traits. "Gee," I said. "I'm not sure what to do about this."

"We weren't too sure, either."

"Let's just see if he can make it through the night, and I'll call somebody first thing in the morning."

"Okay."

"Listen, kids, I'm sorry about this. Hope it's not disturbing for you."

They stared back, not disturbed at all.

"Sure you won't have nightmares?"

"No—of course not."

"Well, then get some sleep now."

In the morning, the wise soul who years before had counseled me on enemas informed me that a lamb could indeed be born without its digestive tract's small-but-crucial terminus. This was a rare developmental defect, but it *did* happen—it had happened on her farm, in fact, several years ago. She had dragged her case to an ambitious vet who proposed to create an anus—surgically—for a sum of money that dwarfed the baby creature's value. In a gesture of dubious humaneness, she had gone along; a few days later, the manufactured orifice became infected and stopped working. Her advice to me was to resolve the situation with the obvious measure, and I did—out behind the barn, while the kids were eating breakfast.

"Get your problem solved?" asked Ethan when I came back in the house.

"Yes."

"How?" Anaïs asked.

Truth, after all, is best. "Well," I told them, "that particular lamb is no longer with us."

Ethan nodded. "What I figured."

"Too bad, Daddy," said Anaïs with touching concern for the old man's feelings. "But don't be too sad, okay? We know it wasn't your fault."

"Thanks. I'm awfully proud of you kids—watching the barn all by yourselves, like that. Seems like you know what to do out there as well as I do."

"Better," Ethan told me. I laughed and took it as a promise.

Critters

By the time Anaïs had turned four years old, she already owned five examples of a toy called My Little Pony. Then she visited the house of a child who owned *fifty* of the things. She left that stable with renewed ambition, and I left wanting to buy stock in the company. My Little Pony proved a toy of outright genius, wedding the natural affinity of little girls to all things equine with their simultaneous fixation on combing hair. On grooming. Each pony came with its own comb and brush; Anaïs spent countless afternoons currying the wild manes and flowing tails on her band of pygmy horses.

It was all just training, though, for the fascinating game of forging relationships with living, breathing animals. Once we let her try her hand at real critters, Anaïs's toy ponies languished on her bedroom shelf. Nowadays, getting along with animals is one of her chief pursuits.

In the valley we call home, critters come in a variety of shapes and sizes; some are wild, some domestic, and some seem quite undecided. Some of them participate directly in our livelihood, and others pose an ongoing threat to our attempts at farming. Looked at from one perspective, much of what we do here is to manage the fortunes of animals—or try to—whether it means keeping sheep in clover, keeping woodchucks out of the corn, or keeping wild predators away from baby lambs. Most of the time I find these efforts unromantic, but to children each transaction can be fraught with high excitement. Children *talk* to animals, and look at them right in the eye, and often manage to engage them with an interest and affection that can make me feel inattentive, bored, and jaded—and, in the most impoverished way, *grown up.*

Why are kids so attracted to critters? At first, I imagined that it might be because of the warmth and pile and texture of the surfaces of animals. Or the way they carry themselves; since children work so hard to master their own locomotion, surely they would take delight in watching other creatures' grace and comfort with their bodies. Maybe it had to do with a dream of independence. Children, after all, know keenly how much they rely on grown-ups, but even a field mouse is skilled at fending for itself. Perhaps it was the desire to communicate, transcending apparent limitations of our human discourse.

I don't think it's anything so complicated, anymore. Children fall for animals because they understand precisely how much human beings are like them—housepets and livestock and full-fledged wildlife, too. How we all fear pain, and strive for joy, and take what steps we can to contrive our own endurance. How our lives are constantly informed by feelings. Thoughts. Emotions. How, within the breast of every kid and critter—even grown-ups—lies a living, beating heart.

Here, then, are stories about life after the era of My Little Pony. I mean, life among the real critters.

Furry Kink

Couples who have not yet made the plunge into parenthood can often be found caring for a pet or two—not precisely as surrogate children, but surely as a vehicle for testing the depths of their nurturing instincts. After two adults conspire to produce a child, though, they discover how quickly infants can usurp the role of family pet. Cats may slink off to find more attentive homes, and overly demonstrative dogs may finally be disciplined into restraining their affections and behaving themselves. Some young families, faced with caring for a human baby, find themselves getting rid of housepets altogether.

Babies need round-the-clock attention and endless care; they can prove to be extremely costly, demanding "pets." But unlike any other pet, babies soon enough grow up and metamorphose into children. When they do, they're apt to yearn for warm, furry critters of their own to cuddle and feed and clean up after.

Since we have no shortage of animals on our sheep farm, Cheryl and I had no conventional cause to offer our children pets. "You want to hug something?" I used to tell first Ethan, then Anaïs. "Just walk out into the pasture and catch a lamb." Catching lambs is easier said than done, but the effort gave our kids the happy illusion that they were playing with animals. Enjoying their company. Expressing affection toward them.

Eventually, the children ceased to find much pleasure in trying to catch the odd lamb and sometimes petting one. What they desired— what was missing—was a sense of ownership for some particular animal. An obvious solution was to give each of them their very own lamb, out of the eight or ten orphans that we raise each spring on artificial milk. "Bottle lambs"—like the one that followed Mary to school in the nursery rhyme—become firmly attached to the person who feeds them and will beg to spend each waking moment in that person's company.

I foresaw several problems with giving orphan lambs to Ethan and Anaïs. First and foremost, lambs make terrible housepets; they tend to be noisy, unsanitary, and destructive. Second, lambs turn into sheep; a well-adjusted sheep must have a reasonable bond with its ovine compatriots, to ensure that the flock behaves as a gregarious unit. Bottle lambs, therefore, are raised with other bottle lambs in their own pen in the barn. Denied mothers, they get bonded to each other—a not-perhaps-ideal but workable route to adult mental health. Lavishing human affection on a bottle lamb only boosts its chances of becoming a screwed-up sheep.

Finally—no laughing matter—any bottle lamb stands a better-than-average chance of infant mortality. Its diet of artificial milk must be provided in specific quantities and at consistent temperatures on quite a rigid schedule, lasting four weeks or longer. If someone skips a feeding or gets careless mixing powder, bottle lambs can lie down and die with appalling ease. Even as a grown-up, I have known pangs of remorse when a bottle lamb is found cold and stiff at feeding time. What thoughtful parent would risk burdening a child's conscience with such a loss?

So orphan lambs as pets were out. On the other hand, by the time Ethan had turned ten and Anaïs five years old, they seemed capable of handling one of the several daily feedings of the bottle lambs. Mixing up the powdered milk, rinsing out the rubber nipples, warming the bottles in hot water on the stove, carrying them to the barn, and feeding one to each lamb—why couldn't our kids do that? Not at midnight, not at six a.m., but why couldn't they take the evening feeding off their parents' hands?

Cheryl argued that it was too much responsibility; when I scoffed, she raised another problem to consider. A pen of bottle lambs, bored to distraction except for periodic binges on milk, can easily degenerate from well-mannered behavior into perfectly weird, socially disturbed perversions that young children ought perhaps not witness. Mimicry of coitus is routinely employed to establish a pecking order from the biggest, most dominant orphan down to the most grovelingly submissive; worse, lambs starved for a mother's teat to suckle will find other, analogous parts of their pen-mates' bodies on which to satisfy the longing to nurse. I'm not talking about thumbsucking, either. Once hooked on fellatio, an especially athletic and twisted and randy lamb may even learn to perform it on himself—but this was not behavior which Cheryl was eager to explain to a five-year-old.

As an interim measure, she proposed that we get housepets for Ethan and Anaïs. Like newlyweds testing their child-rearing instincts on some unsuspecting dog or cat, she suggested, we could study whether our offspring seemed capable of sustained, dedicated caring for animals. Then, given time and increasingly mature perspective, we might work the kids into simple, wholesome barn chores. Like feeding hay or keeping several water buckets filled.

Fine, I said. Housepets. Why not?

Within days, a young kitten and a middle-aged dwarf rabbit had invaded our domestic tranquility. The kitten, feisty runt of a streetwise litter reared in a nearby dairy barn, discouraged all efforts at conventional affection. The rabbit—an extremely nervous, high-strung, Type A bunny—would hop off at lightning speed whenever anyone came near. After just a single morning, I found neither of these animals amusing. Also I found rabbit droppings everywhere and occasional dollops of thick, milky rabbit urine.

"Ethan," I said. "Don't most rabbits live in cages?"

"They told me he was toilet trained."

"Who did?"

"At the pet store. Rabbits are completely fastidious, they said."

"This one seems to be completely incontinent, too."

"What does incontinent mean?" asked Anaïs.

"It means lacking in self-restraint."

"What does *that* mean?"

"Look—" I said as several more brown pellets emerged onto the carpet. "*That* is incontinence."

"You mean always going to the bathroom?"

"That," I told her, "is a euphemism."

"You should have seen his cage at the pet store," said Ethan. "All his mess was piled up in one tiny corner, way across from his food and water."

"Very intelligent."

"I'll bet he's looking for a place he likes right now, Dad. After he chooses, I'll spread newspapers down. And then you'll see: he'll go there every time."

The whole point, I remembered, was to foster in our children the ability to care for critters; since the experiment seemed to be succeeding, I kept my protests muted. Still, after two weeks the rabbit—now christened Balcazar—had failed to choose his proverbial corner of our very large cage. Cleaning up after him had gotten rather boring. As for the relationship between him and the kitten—now christened Asha—there was none to speak of. They loathed each other. Anytime the rabbit came close, the kitten would display an arched back, bared claws, and hypodermic teeth. The rabbit would thump his hind legs, then speed off in some unpredictable direction.

That was life at our house for perhaps a month. Then, one

unforgettable morning, everything changed. I rose from bed at a pre-dawn hour, went downstairs to brew coffee, and beheld, on the kitchen floor, the dwarf rabbit raping this sexually innocent, impressionable feline. The kitten did not seem to be protesting. I stared at this disturbing scene for maybe half a minute, then returned to bed badly shaken. "Cheryl," I whispered. "Asha and Balcazar are making friends."

"That's nice, dear."

It wasn't long before this furry couple had one kinky thing on their minds, and nothing else. All day, all night long. On the sofa, on the stairs, in the hall, the bathroom, the linen closet—everywhere. You could almost hear them challenging each other. "Let's go try it on the rocking chair!" Balcazar would ingeniously propose—and then one could watch them sneak away to keep this assignation. They even developed an elaborate mating dance: Asha would strut with waving tail, then stretch out, coy; Balcazar would thump his hind feet loudly, then spring atop the kitten and pin her with soft, furry forepaws and sheer force of personality.

In the house where *I* grew up, such behavior would have scandalized the owners of these pets. Kids today are cool, though. "They're just mating," Anaïs would casually explain to dumbstruck visitors. Then her fifth-grade brother would add: "It has to do with DNA, you know? And sperm, I think." For a while, we all feared their coupling might produce a monster, but in time we came to doubt their procreative competence. They just seemed to be in it for the kicks; Asha, at any rate, was decidedly prepubescent. One thing was certain: after several hundred occasions of studying this odd pair in flagrante delicto, there was nothing we had to fear allowing our kids to see in the barn.

One day, someone left the front door of the house open and the inevitable happened. Balcazar hopped off, never to be seen again. We mourned the rabbit's disappearance for awhile—Asha mourned, especially—but nothing could be done. A few weeks later, the kitten reached an age deemed appropriate, according to a cat book, for sterilizing. I made an appointment to have her spayed and delivered her to the local veterinarian. "Take it out!" I charged the man. "She's young, but she's already had enough fun to last a lifetime."

"You can pick her up tomorrow," said the good man, and then he saw me to the door.

Couple hours later, the telephone rang. "You the fellow brought a cat in here for spaying?" asked a young assistant to the vet.

"Right," I said. "Asha. Sexy little kitten."

"We've got Asha open on the table right now, but we can't find any ovaries."

Surprise, surprise. "What do you mean, no—"

"Asha turns out to be a boy. I guess we learned the hard way. Now the doctor wonders, do you want to have him castrated?"

I paused to think, but not for long. "Yes, go ahead."

"No charge for opening him up. This is kind of funny, though—don't you think?"

"I'm laughing my head off."

"You can pick him up tomorrow."

I retrieved Asha with a disgusted, grossed-out feeling; the cat outgrew its youthful follies, though, and became a sedate feline with a bent for Proustian reflection, stretched out and purring on the well-worn sofa. Not long after, I succeeded in getting Ethan and Anaïs to undertake a few simple chores for me in the barn. Whatever strange behavior they saw or looked away from down there, on their daily rounds, they were too smart to come to me about it. But after all my fears, they did seem well equipped with the character traits required to give proper care to furry little creatures. Gentleness and patience and respect. Concern—love, even. And the open, wide-eyed attentiveness of true voyeurs. Balcazar and Asha had trained my children well.

Eaten Alive

For many years I have subscribed to *National Wool Grower*, an official magazine of the U.S. shepherding trade. Since most of my fellow shepherds are Westerners, the *Wool Grower* tends to reflect their special concerns and political agenda, which are often not *my* concerns or *my* agenda. One of this journal's long-running themes has been that wild predators—specifically, coyotes—are killing up to one lamb in five on the open range, driving embattled ranchers right out of business. Predator populations are exploding, it is claimed; the real culprits, though, are effete, know-nothing, coyote-loving, urbanite advocates of "environmentalism" who have romanticized these killers and lobbied to restrict the use of various lethal measures by which they might be controlled.

National Wool Grower is the only forum I'm aware of in which "environmentalist" is used like a four-letter word. Since I think of *myself* as an environmentalist, it amuses me to see this magazine next to *Audubon* on my coffee table. One need not be in love with coyotes, I used to say, to accept the role of predation in a stable, balanced ecosystem. Surely with such measures as appropriate fencing, guard dogs, and wary shepherds, predation losses in Wyoming ought to be as manageable as on my farm in Vermont—which was to say, there should be no losses whatsoever.

That was my attitude until the summer of 1986; looking back, it strikes me as comically naive. The trouble started one warm, carefree night when the four of us went for a boat ride on Lake Champlain. Arriving home after dark, I was surprised to see our eighty ewes and one hundred lambs bunched up on the gravel driveway—two pastures away from where I had left them grazing. Notwithstanding their shocked state, we managed to crowd them through a gate into the barnyard. Since no more could be accomplished for them in the dark, we went to bed. Crack of dawn, I rose and took a walk around the farm.

In the abstract, predation seems an unaffecting concept: just a matter of one animal going out to dinner on another. In the real world of shepherding, though, these are seldom neat and tidy meals. What happens is that the predator bites a lamb's throat, then shakes it around until it dies of suffocation or loss of blood...or else manages to tear itself free with a ragged tracheotomy. The ones that get away—and I found three of them, that gray morning—can stagger around for a day or two, bleating for their moms and enduring heartbreaking pain before their expiration. As for the lamb killed outright—only one, typically, in any given coyote strike—it is opened at the gut and various high-protein organs are consumed. Quite unlike a dog, the coyote's taste in lamb runs toward liver, not loin chops. Kidneys, not crown roast. Almost all the red meat goes to waste or to turkey vultures.

There was an older ewe, too, that morning, lying on the hill in the classic stargazing posture. Not a mark was on her. I suppose she died of fright.

I shared my unhappiness over these losses with the Great Pyrenees dog whose job is to guard our sheep from predators. "Where were *you?*" I asked Ginger sharply, and she answered with a sheepish look. Sleeping, I supposed. She paced round and round the carcass, sniffing, taking pains to leave her scent, and I could see she felt just terrible about what happened. But I was running the flock on a large pasture—fifteen acres—and sometimes the dog could be a long way from her grazing charges. Napping. What I didn't know, yet, was that a coyote eating on the run can penetrate a fence, do its surgical business, and be gone inside ten minutes. And be quiet about it, too.

The next strike came one night a week later. Trying to make the dog's presence more effective, I had built new fences to reduce the pasture's size by one-half; although this was inconvenient, it had seemed a wise precaution. No dice. The second kill took place within a hundred yards of my house, and I never heard a sound. I doubt Ginger did, either.

The third strike came a few days later. I don't know exactly what time—I was on my tractor, haying—but it had to be in broad daylight. I was now taking extraordinary pains to pen the whole flock in the barn each night, drastically limiting their daily grazing time. Still, I managed to lose another lamb. My best efforts as a shepherd were serving only to keep a coyote fat and happy.

It is hard to describe the sense of helplessness, defeat, and utter despair that repeated coyote attacks foster in a shepherd. A very weak analogy is finding that raccoons have beaten one to the snow peas in the garden. But cultivating vegetables does not require spending many sleepless nights managing obstetric care and nurturing maternal bonds and patiently getting each tiny, fragile living thing off to an auspicious start. And vegetables do not require daily, dedicated care; they do not bleat in love or in fear; they do not leap and gambol and dance across an emerald field. The sheer economic loss was mightily depressing, too. Each lamb represented seventy-odd dollars in farm income that would not be realized. Expenses, though, would stay about the same. I was getting eaten alive.

At some point during my growing depression, I chatted with a neighboring dairy farmer. "You been having coyote trouble?" he asked.

"I'll say. Something terrible."

"They're all around here this year. Killed a newborn heifer calf last week—and *that's* money."

"Where'd they come from?" I asked.

"Been moving into Vermont since the Sixties, folks say. Nobody cared at first. Now they make you sit right up and notice. Ever seen one?"

"No."

"When you do, you'll know what *wild* means. You ever hear them singing at night?"

"Sometimes—far off, in the distance. It sounds like the end of civilization."

He nodded. "You come across that university fellow yet?"

"Who?"

"That research guy. Drives a blue pickup truck. He's been coming down this road once or twice a day lately."

"Doing what?"

"This guy traps coyotes and then he puts a collar on them. *Radio* collars. That can *transmit*. Then he turns the coyotes *loose* again. He puts on these headphones and he holds up this antenna, and the coyotes tell him where they are. How do you like *that* for research?"

"You mean he's got coyotes who can broadcast? While they eat my lambs?

"Fellow says he figures there's three thousand coyotes in Vermont now. He's got thirty of them he can tune in, anytime."

"He must be some kind of trapper."

"I guess. But if *I* trapped a coyote, I don't think I'd turn it loose. You know what he asked me? He asked me to give him back his collar, if I shoot one. Each of those radio collars costs four hundred bucks."

It wasn't many more days before I came across the blue pickup, parked within a stone's throw of my driveway on a quiet Sunday morning. "I've heard about you," I told the friendly man in headphones.

He repositioned his antenna. "This your sheep farm?" he asked.

"Yes. And boy, am I in trouble."

"You're telling me. You want to listen to Morticia?"

"Who?"

"Morticia. I always liked 'The Addams Family'—you remember that TV show? Been a good source of names for coyotes." He handed me the headphones and I listened to an electronic click on an assigned frequency. Somewhere in the middle distance off to our east, a coyote was broadcasting.

"I would love to see Morticia dead."

The researcher was not surprised to hear it. "Maybe you want her mate, though. Fester."

"I'll take either one," I said, realizing I was talking to a man who had trapped them both.

"You'll need a stroke of luck—these are two successful coyotes. But even if you killed them, it wouldn't make a lot of difference."

"Why?"

"Another pair would move right in to claim the territory. Seems to be running about ten square miles per family. This whole county's all staked out, from their point of view. You create a vacancy, it won't take them long to fill it."

He noted Morticia's compass bearing on a pad, then climbed into the truck to drive ahead and get a reading from another point. Like plotting a forest fire: where the two readings intersected, there would be his coyote. He would jot down her position and file it for future reference, building a composite picture of her territory.

"Let me get this right," I said. "You're telling me to give up hope."

"I'm telling you that coyotes are here to stay. They *like* it here. They're doing well. Farmers who can't keep their livestock safe are going to lose them."

I went home and perused old copies of the *National Wool Grower* with renewed interest. There were references to marksmen who could work from light airplanes; there were long articles about fitting lambs with collars that release a toxic compound when a coyote makes its characteristic throat-kill. There were ads for vials of expensive coyote urine that might help lure the predators to traps. With enough time and money and determination, one could probably kill a coyote; but it seemed irrelevant, given the wider perspective of an endless supply of coyotes eager to call this attractive valley home.

After the next kill, I gave up on pasture-based lamb production. I weaned every lamb on the premises and set out to feed them in the safety of the barn—a poor economic choice when one has lush pastures and heavy-milking ewes, but the only choice when lambs are being gobbled like potato chips. Several lambs proved neither old enough nor large enough to tolerate weaning and promptly died of malnutrition. Three ewes, too, developed severe mastitis for having their lambs removed on short notice. At least predation losses ceased: apparently a 130-pound sheep is not the prey of choice for a 40-pound coyote.

By autumn, everybody in my neck of the woods had a gruesome coyote story to tell; tempers were running high. Then deer hunters—and, later, snowmobilers—stumbled onto various dens and summarily executed the inhabitants. Nights grew quiet for a time. I suspected, though, that our relief would be short-lived. Sure enough, by lambing season we would wake up in the night and hear the eerie coyote songs again.

With the onset of the next grazing season, I replaced my entire fencing system with new, state-of-the-art materials. The current fence is a portable netting made of plastic twine and stainless steel wire; the battery-powered fence charger that electrifies it can spit out 7000 volts.

We never enclose more than an acre at a time, nowadays, and every couple days we *move the fence* to enclose the next itty-bitty pasture. In so confined a paddock, even a narcoleptic guard dog like ours seems able to defend her turf.

The new system means a couple hundred hours of fence-moving labor every year, but it has absolutely stopped predation. Other meals, for the time being, must be easier for the coyotes who were dining on our lambs. Still, I scarcely feel optimistic for the long haul; over the next decade, coyotes may well doom New England's pasture-based systems of livestock production, with profound consequences on land-use patterns and the pastoral "look" of places like Vermont.

I know one thing, anyway: these days, when I pick up the *National Wool Grower*, the outraged stories about western-style predation strike a sympathetic chord. Why indeed should shepherds knock themselves out to feed this gourmet fare to coyotes? Small wonder that sheep numbers in the U.S. have been dropping steadily. Shepherds quit, demoralized and beaten by the predator. My advice to effete, know-nothing, coyote-loving, urbanite advocates of "environmentalism": eat those lamb chops while you can.

Out of the Bag

Four winters ago, while cross-country skiing through some woods adjacent to my farm, I came across the large tracks of an unfamiliar critter who must have recently gone bounding through the snow. *Large* tracks. Ginger, our Great Pyrenees guard dog, tips a scale at 115 pounds— but I doubted that even her enormous feet could have made these paw prints. Besides, she never leaves the flock's well-fenced winter paddock. More amazing still, these tracks had been impressed into the snow at intervals of four to five feet: the animal that made them had been moving right along.

There must be a dog around here bigger than our own, I thought. I made a mental note—soon enough forgotten—and skied back home.

Prior to this time, I had never understood the excitement expressed by so many on catching mere glimpses of creatures in the wild. Deer, for example. People in Vermont—and I mean natives just as well as tourists—tend to go nuts over sighting the odd white-tail. One sees a buck or doe for a fleeting second, flying through the woods; bearing witness to such an event can dominate a person's conversation for the next full week.

And should a deer manage to distinguish itself as an individual—let alone a pet—the wildlife claque may go totally berserk. It happened in our county in the spring of 1987, when a doe named Bonkers made repeated front-page headlines. Illegally raised from fawnhood in captivity, unafraid of human or automotive traffic, Bonkers roamed the backroads of several nearby towns wearing a red collar and availing herself of countless photo opportunities. Then she started tagging along with a local jogger and the jogger's Malamute on their daily workouts. The jogger became unamused: Bonkers would consistently force the athlete to break stride, and occasionally she would playfully attack the dog. A complaint was filed with the Fish and Wildlife Commissioner, and soon enough Bonkers found herself inside the deer paddock at Santa's Land, a petting zoo in Putney.

Then all hell broke loose. Fish and Wildlife telephones rang off their hooks, thousands of names were gathered on petitions, and the Memorial Day parade in Middlebury could have been mistaken for a protest march demanding LET OUR BONKERS GO! Caving in to unrelenting pressure, state officials pulled the doe out of Santa's Land and gave her a one-way boat ride to a private island in Lake Champlain. One measly Vermont deer, out of a herd estimated at 100,000, had been turned into a public cause célèbre.

Or take the case of the moose—the world-famous moose—that wandered out of the woods surrounding Shrewsbury, Vermont (pop. 600), in the fall of 1986 to woo a cow named Jessica. The moose had One Thing on his mind; 60,000 human voyeurs dropped by, in the next few weeks, to snap photos and cheer him on. If Larry Carrara, who happened to own Jessica, had previously thought he understood the meaning of his life—something to do with running a farm, say—he now must have wondered if he'd been mistaken. What if all his years had been mere prelude for a life of showmanship, of playing spokesperson for a large, wild, lovestruck beast, and of jumping both-feet-first into the roadside souvenir business?

Many poems have been written; dozens of clever journalistic pieces have been penned; droves of photographers who made the trek to Shrewsbury have secured glossy, visual documentation of this offbeat affair. In time, the moose departed: after ten weeks of constant badgering by paparazzi, I imagine that the honeymoon seemed over. One of romantic life's more difficult amours, the sort of test of character no man or moose can quite prepare for. And who would wish such a complicated situation on another living creature, whether wild or not?

So although I had never placed myself among the first rank of wildlife enthusiasts, I was sorely tempted within months of finding those tracks in the snow. On a chilly April morn, while tightening slack fences in what amounts to my farm's back forty, I looked up to see a cat striding boldly through the meadow not two hundred yards away. A cat—golden-yellow fur, long tail, cat head, catlike muscling and bearing and gait. And then, as the cat calmly disappeared into the woods, it hit me: any housecat at that distance would have been the merest speck on the horizon. This feline had proportions that a housecat might assume when viewed across the back lawn, not a sprawling hayfield.

I went home and confided to Cheryl: "Remember those gigantic tracks last winter? In the snow?"

"What about them?"

"I think they were made by a panther."

"What?"

"A mountain lion. It sounds crazy, but I just now saw one."

Cheryl frankly disbelieved me; two weeks later, though, I saw the cat again. It was evening. I was sitting on the deck outside our house, and the cat was stalking through a meadow on the far side of our pond—150 yards away—collaring unlucky field mice and popping them down like junk food. I stared, open-mouthed, feeling the feverish excitement that novice hunters confess on finding their first buck in the crosshairs of a rifle scope. Then I ran into the house to call my wife and kids; by the time I herded them onto the deck, the cat was gone.

I visited a local wildlife buff and asked him if we still had mountain lions in Vermont.

"If we do," he told me, "they are scarcer than hen's teeth. Last *recorded* sighting was at least forty years ago."

"How do you record a sighting?"

"Take a sharp photograph. Or shoot the cat and show the carcass."

"I don't own a camera," I said. "And I'm not a hunter, either. But I swear to God, I've seen a mountain lion on my farm."

He went to his refrigerator and pulled out two bottles of beer from a recently opened Vermont brewery. *Catamount,* read the label right next to a drawing of the head of my beast. "Look anything like this?"

"That's it. That's my critter."

"Golly, I would love to see that!"

"You don't think I'm crazy, do you?"

"No, I don't. Not personally. No reason why there shouldn't still be a few around. Plenty of wilderness left in Vermont. Plenty of deer to feed on. But if I were you, I'd keep my mouth shut."

"Why?"

"An awful lot of people would consider that a trophy."

We drank up, and I went home to explore the cliffs that define my farm's boundaries to the south and east. There were shallow caves aplenty and deep fissures that I dared not plumb. I climbed out onto one ledgy precipice that was littered with piles of well-cleaned bones; suddenly I got the willies and the disturbing sensation of being watched. I scrambled down the rocky face, then sprinted for the open meadow. No panther came bounding after me, claws bared. But I decided to avoid cliff prowls in future, just as I avoid expeditions to Kenya.

And then, just a few evenings later, came the group sighting. Cheryl and I were sitting in the house enjoying drinks with two other couples—dinner guests—when somebody looked up and pointed to the distant pond. "What kind of an animal is *that*?" our friend asked.

"That," I said, "is our new mascot. Seems to be a mountain lion."

At first none of them believed me, but the cat gave us a good ten minutes to study it at distances from 150 to 300 yards. I found Anaïs's field glasses, too, and we passed the binoculars from hand to hand while staring at the big kitty's unconcerned play. No question about it: we were looking at a great, big cat. It would crouch in tall grass, then spring and pounce on real or imagined prey; it would saunter, carefree as you like, along the water's edge. And then, in the gathering dusk, the feline wandered back into the woods from whence it came.

"That is just astounding!"

"I would like it," I suggested, "if we all just kept this to ourselves. Okay? I don't want 60,000 people up here, lion hunting. I don't want this cat to be the next Shrewsbury moose or another Bonkers."

"But—my God, a mountain lion!"

"Let's just keep it quiet, okay?"

I think I succeeded in swearing them to secrecy but it never mattered. I saw the catamount only once more, a few days later, before it disappeared for good. Gone without a trace: no tracks, no sightings, no evening mousing exhibitions in the meadow by the pond. Probably moved on to better hunting grounds, and I'm sure it's just as well—all for the better, even. But I get a little wistful when I think of what a puss I had, and what a puss I lost. And nowadays, when I hear others chatter in excitement about sighting wild critters, I can understand.

Heartaches

In her ninth year, Anaïs finally obtained a horse. For months she had devoted each spare moment to fundraising activities—yard sales, a lemonade stand, a dog walking service, outright begging—to raise enough money to buy a horse. Then, in a stroke of fortune, I opened a farmers' newspaper and spied an advertisement for *free* horses. They were on loan from September until June, from a summer camp thirty miles away. Now Anaïs roams the farm on an aging pony named Doodles, an animal of splendid disposition and extensive experience with horse-struck little girls. And my daughter's piggy bank has been preserved intact.

Anaïs's cat, however, sensed a displacement of affection from the moment the horse van lumbered up the gravel driveway. Little had Asha guessed that in his four-year residence here, he had served Anaïs as something in between My Little Pony and the real thing. Something warm to feed and care for, something soft to stroke and talk to. Now that the real thing was right here on the premises, Asha's shortcomings became all too apparent. You can give a cat commands, but who really expects it to obey? You can call a cat, but no response is ever guaranteed. And, unless you are a flea, you cannot climb onto a cat's furry saddle and go for a ride. This last drawback placed Asha at a serious disadvantage to Doodles.

The cat's first response was to mope around the house, whining. Then he would skulk outside between the back door and the pasture, poised to intercept Anaïs each time she set out to pay a visit to Doodles. And finally, when all else had failed, the cat transformed himself from a reflective, unambitious, laid-back sort of feline into Asha the Terrible, scourge of every field mouse within a short prowl of our house. Not only would he mercilessly hunt these rodents down, he would carry their half-flayed bodies onto our front porch and leave them on the sisal mat, where we wipe our dirty feet. *Love me!* he seemed at evident pains to urge us. But it was an unbecoming way to welcome people home.

As for those unlucky mice, I hold that each one died on account of Asha's aching heart.

Something similar happened to our woodchucks. All summer long we used to watch them from a distance—a mating pair, we liked to think—scuttling from the garden after ravaging the beans or corn. These depredations were annoying but not too expensive. Come autumn, though, the woodchucks set up shop beneath the grain bin where I store the pelleted feed we buy to grow our lambs from 60-pound weanlings into 110-pound gourmet treats. I knew the woodchucks were under there, because I would see their beady little eyes peering out from beneath the oak rails that support the plywood bin. I knew it because any grain I spilled, while filling pails at chore time, would be thoroughly cleaned up before the next day's feeding. I knew it because those woodchucks learned to work the sheet-metal gate—about the size of a four-by-six-inch index card—that allows grain to cascade out of the bin. Each time they jiggled the handle on this sliding plate, gravity would offer them a bountiful reward. They learned quickly. They learned well. I was their meal ticket.

One of the strengths of American agriculture is that a relatively small proportion of our grain crop winds up in the mouths of vermin. Decades of investment have left us with expensive facilities—climate-controlled steel bins and concrete elevators—that keep the precious harvest safe from hungry little mouths. In societies where farming methods are not so advanced, the inadvertent feeding of rodents results in major crop losses. There was no way I could quantify how much grain I was losing to this pair of woodchucks, but it seemed manifestly un-American to let them help themselves to feed destined for others, feed that I had bought and paid for.

My little grain bin is not an expensive storage facility. I built it ten years ago for $115. It's eight feet long and four feet wide and six feet high—plus gable roof—and it looks like an ice-fishing shanty with no door or windows. When I order grain, a huge truck comes to the farm and blows three tons of pellets up a six-inch filler pipe into the bin. When no more grain will fit, the driver hands me a bill for about $600. Over the next few weeks, gravity allows most of those pellets to flow freely out the sliding gate, which is built into one of the endwalls. Then the day comes when no more grain will flow, so I crack the roof and climb inside the bin to shovel the remaining pellets toward the hole.

Imagine my astonishment, one crisp autumn morning, when I pried up a section of the grain bin's roof and stared down at a frightened woodchuck right *inside* the bin. As the level of grain had lowered until the pellets would no longer flow freely out the open gate, I imagine this explorer squeezed his way inside...and then the gate dropped shut behind him. He looked mighty well fed. On the American plan, so to speak.

I eyed the woodchuck, and he eyed me, and I watched him weigh his fight-or-flight options. They were few indeed. Recognizing that he had nowhere to run, he backed into a corner of the bin and bared his long, sharp teeth. I strolled to the house to get a gun.

I am not, by any stretch of the imagination, a hunter; the gun on this farm—an ancient .22—is on long-term loan from my brother-in-law, who lives in Texas. I doubt the rifle had been fired in the half-dozen years before I took it down from its shelf and checked its laborious bolt-lock, single-shot action. Then I had to search to find where I had hidden the box of bullets. Twenty minutes later, I approached the grain bin feeling like some Green Mountain Wyatt Earp. Loaded for ground hog. I climbed up the two-by-four ribs along the bin's sidewall and poked my head inside. The woodchuck had not moved. With the roof cracked open only a foot or so, I was unable to sight directly down the barrel at my quarry's head. But I poked the rifle in his general direction, took aim as best I could, and gently squeezed the trigger.

This should have been no more difficult than harpooning a trout in a goldfish bowl, but the fact is that my first shot went well wide of its mark. Chalk it up to woodchuck fever. The sharp report shocked us both, however, and I staggered backwards from my perch and landed on the ground. I ejected the spent casing, reloaded the rifle, then climbed up and took aim, and missed the woodchuck once again. By now he was in a state of frozen terror, and I wasn't feeling all that great myself. The problem, I knew, was that the angle of the grain bin's roof interfered with my taking careful aim. So I got a ladder and a crowbar, pried off a four-foot section of the roof, and climbed to where I had an unobstructed field of vision. BLAM! One of my pair of nemeses would steal no more.

Two days later, the other woodchuck was found flattened in the road, run down by some speeding car. All right, I can't *prove* it was the buddy of the one I blasted; but my grain bin is no longer serving uninvited guests. And what could cause a wily, well-fed woodchuck with a home beneath a three-ton cornucopia to wander out onto the highway? It doesn't take an animal psychologist to guess that this creature died of a broken heart.

I don't know what other shepherds do with tired, wornout rams, but we tend to keep ours on the premises until they drop. Unlike the meat of older ewes, theirs is so strongly flavored as to be of little value. Years ago, we slaughtered one such ram and couldn't get even the dog to eat it. Even in their dotage, though, rams can grow enough wool in a year to cover their expenses. And in an emergency—as when some flashy young buck can't deliver the goods—there are ways to coax old rams into yet one more round of breeding.

Recently, we had two such old boys on our hands for a couple years after we had stopped counting on them for stud services. One we simply called the Dorset, but his Suffolk buddy had the honorific title Mister Right. Both rams had impressive pedigrees, and both had arrived on the farm in 1983. They were rivals from the start, bashing heads and charging each other and carrying on as though locked in mortal combat. Turned out together into our flock of ewes, this pair could accomplish nothing. Each ram was so concerned the other one might sire a lamb that he would waste his strength in shoving matches and displays of male prowess. Eventually we learned to split the flock in half at breeding time and give each ram his private harem.

The smaller of these rams—the Dorset—started showing signs of aging long before his Suffolk partner. He had a nasty tendency to stomach bloat, and a chronic rivulet of snot dribbled from one nostril. By 1988 there was little fight left in him, and the Suffolk ram appeared the victor in their long-fought battle. The Suffolk's lust for mating was no longer indefatigable, but he looked in fine condition even as his rival went downhill before our eyes. Each day, the Dorset's presence among the living seemed a minor miracle; still, he lived for two more years. And then, one night just last spring, the Dorset ram finally died in his sleep, surrounded by dozens of his wives and scores of offspring.

We do not mourn such losses. That ram had a decent life. Incredibly, Mister Right—his lifelong enemy—expired without any warning scarcely two weeks later. Cardiac arrest? Stroke? Liver malfunction? In all my years of shepherding, I've never seen a sheep contrive to die so quickly. I have my own theory: heartache. Creatures need the love of other creatures, but my hunch is that they come to need their enemies as well. Bereft of a lifelong rival, my Suffolk ram, I imagine, saw little left to live for. Enmity can be an important way of caring, too.

Animals do not live by bread alone. Or by cat food, pelleted grain, or even clover hay. They live by virtue of a web of social interactions—fraught with many styles and varieties of caring—each of which creates a vulnerability to heartache. Even, sometimes, to heart failure. Small wonder that the lives of animals have power to move us: humans can be highly susceptible to heartache, too.

Squatter's Rights

A couple of decades ago, as a near college dropout returning to school at the very last minute, I found myself assigned to share a dormitory room with a young man who took offense when I suggested he get lost, from time to time, so that my girlfriend and I could enjoy sexual congress. Without delving into the merits of his case—*or* mine—let me say that we recognized our incompatibility and together begged a dean to move one of us out. He couldn't, though: the dorms were full. And so, in a classic demonstration of the spirit of the late 1960s, my girlfriend and I borrowed a shovel from a sympathetic professor and set forth into the college arboretum to build ourselves a house—or a hovel, at any rate.

We walked far off the beaten paths, crossed a turbid creek on a fallen log, and eventually found ourselves following a long-abandoned road that meandered through a hardwood forest half a mile from the main campus. Downhill from these twin dirt-tracks, into the side of an embankment rife with shrubs and bushes, we began to dig a hole. Some days later, when the hole was eight feet square and three to four feet deep, we borrowed a car and bought six sheets of plywood to line the hole's dirt walls and top them with a thin, flat roof. Then we backfilled the site, using dirt and twigs and leaves to camouflage our construction so thoroughly that, unless one knew our burrow was hiding there, one could stroll right past it and scarcely have a clue.

That was in September. We lived in that rude hut for the next three months—or we slept there, anyway—feathering our nest with paisley fabrics to cover the waist-high walls, a Coleman lantern to illuminate the odd textbook, and a Coleman stove for heating and cooking needs. As autumn frosts began denuding the trees, however, the leading edge of our rabbit hutch began to emerge from the smooth lines of the landscape. Our field of vision gradually expanded to reveal the ample, well-kept house and grounds of Swarthmore's Vice-President—barely two hundred yards away from us, albeit on the sluggish creek's opposite bank. But if we could peer out and see that stern administrator's home, wouldn't he eventually peer out and see ours?

Then, come December, the dirty creek froze solid. Kids from the local village came out, afternoons, to skate; no matter what we tried to do with leaves and twigs and branches, the entrance to our underground house seemed to poke quite prominently from the frozen earth. Sure enough, over Christmas break our home was violated—utterly trashed, in fact—by juvenile delinquents with no trace of respect for other people's property. They burned holes in our sleeping bag, smeared fecal matter on our Coleman stove, and tore the plywood trapdoor right off its hinges. There was not much left worth saving.

Taking stock, my sweetheart and I saw no choice but to leave the forest. For three idyllic months, we had illegally squatted on the college's private lands; but as squatters whose home had been uncovered—and robbed and ruined—where could we turn for justice? Nowhere. The fact was, we were lucky to have not been apprehended. We moved back into our respective dormitories; six months later, there was only the faintest depression in the ground marking where we had lain as man and wife.

A couple of years later, I married the intrepid young woman who had risked going into the woods with me. A couple of years after that, Cheryl and I thought it might make sense to buy a rundown farm in Vermont, convert a sagging hay barn into our first real house, and try to pose as New Age farmers. It is hard to reconstruct the state of mind that fostered these decisions, but the thought of making ourselves *legal* squatters—landowners—must have exerted a subliminal influence.

On the day a realtor first showed us our dream kingdom, threatening skies prevented us from taking an extensive walk. But the agent placed a Federal Land Bank map in our hands, and back in his office we studied it with mounting interest. Toward the back of the farm's long, somewhat narrow valley—just where the map showed a scruffy meadow fading into unkempt woodlot—a pair of dotted lines marched faintly across the page to mark an old, abandoned road.

"Is that road still there today?" asked Cheryl.

"Well, you couldn't *drive* it. Just two dirt-tracks going through the woods. Snowmobiles use it in the winter. You could ski it, maybe."

"Where does that road go?"

"Nowhere, anymore. Used to be a town road—used to go to Middlebury. There's an oldtimer down on Twitchell Hill who says he used to *plow* that road. With a team of horses. That was sixty years ago, though. After a while, the town just threw it up."

"I beg your pardon?"

"Throwing up a road means the town won't plow it, anymore. Or bring in fresh gravel, or grade it, or clean the culverts—nothing. They just throw it up, you see? Why should taxpayers take care of a road where no one wants to live?"

"I can't think of any reason," I said.

"Right. So it comes before the Town Meeting, and they vote to throw it up. Goes right in the minutes."

"So, like now that road would be part of the farm?" asked Cheryl.

"Sure—but it won't *take* you anywhere, you understand? Now, sometimes you can buy land with an old town road that's *not* thrown up. Or not thrown up legally and proper. It may be abandoned—it may even be all overgrown—but if it's a town road and you build a year-round house along it, you can make the taxpayers put it back in shape for you. Even if it's miles off the beaten track, you can make them fix it so a schoolbus can get in and out. Even in the wintertime—and so they have to plow it, too, you see? So that's some deal, huh?"

I nodded. "That must be incredibly expensive."

"Oh, I guess. That's why a smart town gets its old town roads thrown up. So—you buy that farm I showed you, you'll be moving to a smart town."

We *did* buy the farm he showed us. And, on the sunny autumn day when we took possession, we made an unhurried ramble to assess our new domain. The old town road seemed unaccountably familiar; then I realized that it evoked much of the essence of that other unused road through the far-flung reaches of the Swarthmore arboretum. It, too, climbed gradually through a hardwood grove; it, too, had given up portions of its right-of-way to eager, grasping saplings. With a joyful heart I slipped my hand around my wife's: maybe our abandoned road went nowhere, but it took us back. Walking its length recalled— poignantly, indelibly—a lost umbilicus to our autumn in the woods.

Over several years' time the road grew worse, however. Snowmobilers didn't help it. Neither did rotting elms that kept collapsing onto it of their own considerable accord. Saplings, too, gradually metamorphosed into trees; in places, it became hard to discern where once a road had been. I felt a little guilty, at first, to witness this decay without lifting a finger. But there were numerous demands on my time, and the project of preserving the old town road in a state adequate to nurture personal nostalgia could not be assigned a high priority in my new, demanding agrarian life. The road was disappearing before our very eyes, but all I could do was let it slip away.

Property owners are prone to certain classic nightmares. Chief of these must be the dream in which one learns one does not own exactly what one thought one did; I confess I used to have that bad dream routinely, till our lives grew settled here. Having children helped, I think. But I also used to have another, less common nightmare. In it, I would chance to find illegal squatters on our land—living in some shack or cabin virtually under my unsuspecting nose. Accosting them, I would find out they didn't give a damn about me. Eloquent nihilists, they could rail emotionally against the absurdity of real-estate ownership.

My special problem was that, deep in some heart of hearts, I thought the squatters were right: from the point of view of cosmic justice, how could it be fair that my family should get to "own" this little valley? Sure, we were shelling out a lot of money—mortgage payments, interest, taxes—to earn the legal right to call this farm our home. But in a former era, I had been a squatter, too: I understood too well what personal exigencies might bring otherwise decent individuals to put together a dwelling on land they did not "own." And to scoff at any concept of ownership that outlawed such behavior, especially where land was plainly going unused. Like my unmanaged forests—all sixty acres.

I needed to overcome this disturbing nightmare, and one strategy was to assert greater dominion over all corners of our Ponderosa. To that end, several years ago I signed up with the government to create a conservation plan for the entire farm and gradually implement it. Part of this plan required bulldozing "diversion ditches" into nearly every meadow, at no small cost to the nation's generous taxpayers and myself; one of these ditches was dug with its terminus parallel with the sad remains of the old town road. That, I thought, would utterly destroy the romantic power once evoked by that soft path—but what adult has not cashiered the odd ideal for a better night's sleep? And, after all, progress is progress. The dozers came, and dug, and went, and after that I found myself consciously avoiding the old road each time I set out for a walk.

Until just two years ago. A local lumberjack, while out hunting deer, had admired some red oaks in the far reaches of our woodlot; on his advice, I engaged a private forester to cruise our forest and tell me what timber might be smart to harvest. This expert and I went hiking on a wintry day, and halfway through our tramp we crossed a section of the old town road. It felt like some *déjà vu*—the road was broad, and neat, and darn near totally cleared of both young trees and worthless deadfalls. While I was swallowing my astonishment, the affable forester remarked: "I see you've got some beavers."

"How? Where?"

"Look at these stumps," he said, kicking with his boot at one or two out of hundreds of gnawed-off trees.

"This is news to me," I told him.

"First question is, where did they put their lodge?" He scanned the middle distance and then pointed it out for me, a brown igloo poking from the frozen landscape no less prominently than had our ancient hut in the college arboretum—after the leaves had fallen. "There," he nodded. "Question number two is, where's their dam?"

We took a little walk and, soon enough, he found it: the beavers had thrown an intricate and graceful weir across the big, expensive soil conservation ditch, so that its final couple hundred feet would now hold water permanently—defeating, no doubt, part of the government's carefully engineered purpose in digging it. "Gee," I said. "I'm not sure if I like this—and I know darn well the government's not going to like it."

"Squatters' rights," the forester told me affably. "They were looking for a house site, and I guess you gave them one."

We walked across the frozen pond the beavers had created, and we stood right next to their cunning lodge of mud and sticks. Those little architects were right inside—probably sitting stock-still and listening to our every word. I even thought I knew just what it must be like, inside there: no paisley fabrics, but I knew how such a space could feel. "So how do I get the buggers out?" I asked.

"Dynamite. You blow their dam up, they may go find someplace else to live. But then again, they might rebuild it. Even higher, maybe."

"Higher?"

"Oh, beavers have been known to flood quite a little bit of land."

I looked back to the old town road—now marvelously manicured in consequence of the timber harvest to create this backwoods Venice—and I thought, simultaneously, of some fine print in one of my several contracts with the U.S. Soil Conservation Service. *I agree to maintain this practice for at least ten years...I agree to refund all or part of the cost-share assistance paid to me if before the expiration of the practice lifespan specified, I (a) destroy the practice installed, or (b) relinquish....*

But I snapped out of this legal reverie and looked around me with appropriate wonder. Squatters had—at long last—come to build their hovel on my land, and the scale of their dreams was positively awe-inspiring. Would I now turn cop and bust them? I took a deep, reflective breath. "As far as I'm concerned," I said, "these critters can stay."

Nowadays, whenever Cheryl or I can find a spare half hour, we'll walk back with our kids to check on the beavers. Not that any one of us has seen them—yet—but it feels as though we have. Things change back there constantly. Presumably working in the dead of night, they fell tree after tree and buck them into useful lengths; once transported to the construction zone, they are mortared into place with sticky, well-packed mud. The dam has ably withstood many torrents, as well as spring floods caused by melting snow; never quite satisfied, its furry engineers continue shoring it up further. Ultimately, who knows what these conservation partners have in mind for my land? All I know is, anytime I want to feel indolent I need only hike back to review their latest progress.

One recent evening, in the library of our farmhouse, Ethan and Anaïs were doing some research on our now-welcome squatters. "Beavers live on *bark*," my son informed me, peering up from a heavy encyclopedia. "And they use their *tails* to support themselves while gnawing trees. And they raise their babies up together for the first two years, then they send them out to go build dams and lodges of their own."

I told him I found that just amazing—every bit of it.

Then my daughter, who has learned to study thick books herself, read me a passage from another volume. She said: "Some wildlife biologists think that beavers tend to mate for life."

"What a nice idea!" I told her. I like to think that I have, too.

Improving the Breed

❧❦❧

T he decline of farm culture in my corner of Vermont has been going on, quietly, for quite a few years now. In nearby Middlebury, for example, the building that once housed a Ford tractor dealership is now a small factory that produces plywood cows. Some are nearly life-size. These become lawn ornaments for a growing citizenry that admires icons of agrarian life but hates to smell manure. Folks still like to *speak* of farming as though it were our landscape's fundamental occupation, but each year fewer and fewer Vermonters earn their livings inside barns. Or even peek inside one.

I confess I do not earn my living in a barn, either. I gave it an honest try but found out it would take a lot more sheep than I desired to care for. So we have settled for a flock that is rather more demanding than a sensible hobby, and yet far less remunerative than a real job. Still, our place *needs* animals to keep its fields groomed and open; I suppose we also use our sheep to focus—and to justify—a certain dimension of our rural lives. And so we continue to perform the daily chores of farmers.

In various subtle ways, though, our flock has started mirroring the deterioration—"progress"—we see going on all around us. Where once we specialized in breeding hypersexed, superprolific, heavy-milking ewes, nowadays we're apt to choose the most *undistinguished* lambs to replace the older mothers in our eighty-ewe flock. They may make less money, but these doggedly average ewes also make less trouble for us. They can winter right outdoors, eating hay strewn across the frozen ground and slaking their thirsts with an occasional snowball. They can procreate with their own uncles, fathers—even brothers—without giving birth to hemophiliacs or idiots. They break no production records, but they seldom work themselves into a state of metabolic stress. The way I've come to see it, if God wanted sheep to have triplets he would have given them three teats.

This laid-back philosophy was not acquired overnight, though. We've been through one sort of fire or another with our flock more times than I care to dredge from memory. Lately, though—now that Cheryl and I finally share realistic attitudes toward what we can expect from sheep—we find ourselves plotting to hand the entire flock over to our children. *Soon.* To see what Ethan and Anaïs can accomplish as young shepherds and to let them earn an offbeat line on their resumes. Eighty ewes—a gift outright. I just hope those kids won't think to look them in the mouth.

Inductions

My wife wanted to have our first child at home, but an erratic fetal heartbeat on the evening of her labor forced us to make a midnight dash to the hospital. Midwives and all—with our tails tucked between our legs, so to speak. In went the forceps and out came our son, apparently none the worse for classic cephalopelvic disproportion.

Five years later, and pregnant with our second child, Cheryl and I gave no serious thought to home birth. In the intervening years, we had become shepherds; we had both seen enough malpresented lambs to know how easily the miracle of birth can run amok. When and if it does, home is simply not the place to be.

But on the other hand, Cheryl wanted to give birth as naturally as possible in a hospital setting. No drugs. No I.V. No brightly lit delivery room, if that could be avoided. The hospital's complicated life-support systems were just so much insurance, to be used only if necessary. What she really wanted was a home birth in a hospital.

The baby was due in late March of 1981, and the timing could not have been less felicitous. Our sheep were due to start dropping lambs the very same week, and it was unreasonable to expect much help from Cheryl out in the lambing barn. Still, the situation made for an amusing winter: as Cheryl's belly stretched and sunk and swelled with child, so did those of our woolly, bleating charges.

The Ides of March came and went, and then the vernal equinox. I started penning the ewe flock in the barn at night, the better to keep tabs on them. And then, at evening feeding time on March 25th, a ewe of enormous girth declined to eat her supper. She preferred to pace and paw the floor and practice Lamaze breathing.

Back in our warm house, I told the news to Cheryl: "Bet we get the year's first lambs tonight."

"Really?"

"Got some labor, out there." I waved toward the barn. "And how about you?"

"I guess I'm doing fine," she said.

I checked the barn again at ten o'clock, and then at midnight. Something was quite wrong with the progress of this old ewe's labor. She was working hard, but her contractions were irregular and they seemed to be availing her nothing. So at one o'clock I did what a veterinary seminar had taught me to do: I opened a clean syringe and gave the ewe a shot of estrogen to efface her cervix. And then—half an hour later—I injected her with oxytocin. Then I ran home to warm my hands and brew a pot of coffee.

"Honey?" called Cheryl from the bedroom.

"How come *you're* awake?"

"My water broke half an hour ago." Which is to say her amniotic sac had ruptured.

I went in and hugged Cheryl. "Did you call your doctor?"

"Yes—but I'm not in labor. No contractions yet."

"Well, what did your doctor say?"

"He said to get some sleep and come in first thing in the morning. As long as nothing happens."

"Great," I said, and kissed her.

"It's *not* great. If I don't start contracting spontaneously, he'll want to induce me. With pitocin."

"That's what *I* just did."

"Huh?"

"To that sheep. Well, oxytocin—same thing, right?"

"Hospitals have these obstetric protocols they follow. Once your water breaks, they want the baby out in twenty-four hours."

"Well, don't worry," I said. "You just try to get some rest. I've got to lamb this ewe out now, okay?"

"Okay," she nodded. Cheryl understood the power of oxytocin. Once you give a pregnant ewe a decent shot of it, things start happening fast. The uterus *contracts*. Sometimes lambs can squirt out like a slippery watermelon seed squeezed between two fingers. So I threw my winter jacket on and marched back to the barn.

The ewe was still getting nowhere. I watched for a while, then soaped my hand and forearm and reached into her womb to find out why. Big, goopy trouble: a dead fetus, partially mummified and inauspiciously presented. These things happen—honestly, they do—but why do they always seem to happen at the worst of times? Over the next hour or so, I worked to reposition this pathetic bag of bones such that it could be delivered. And then, once I'd pulled it out, I reached back in to find another lamb. Alive and healthy, this time. I watched the mother lick it clean, then helped it find a teat and gorge itself on first milk.

By the time I stumbled into bed, cold and exhausted and smelling like a uterus, it was awfully late. I nudged Cheryl. "You having contractions?"

"Not yet. How'd your ewe do?"

"Fine," I told her. "Big, strong single lamb."

In the morning, Cheryl was still waiting for the first contraction. We drove to the hospital and she was examined. Her doctor said she ought to stay. He wanted to induce her.

"No," she said, thinking all at once of fifty things she had to get done right away. Important projects. A formal compromise was reached: she could leave till noon and then come back. If her labor hadn't gotten underway by then, she would agree to letting him induce it. We left, and took a long walk in the crisp air and brilliant sunlight. "I don't want those drugs," she told me.

"I know," I said. "But it's not like sheep."

"No?"

"Well, it's not one big injection. It's a tiny, metered drip. I.V."

"Big difference."

I could see her point. No one who has used oxytocin in a lambing barn would compare induced labor to the real thing. It is like comparing a slow, steady, gathering storm to a sudden cloudburst. I was in the middle, though—between the doctor and my wife—and I held Cheryl to her bargain. Shortly after noon, she climbed into a bed in the hospital's labor room and had an I.V. installed in her left arm.

"Don't go in my wrist, okay?" she asked. "I have to knit."

She was, indeed, knitting a pair of booties for the baby. Out of our own wool. The I.V. was installed up near her elbow, so her hands could work. A technician set the pitocin-drip machine to a minuscule rate of dispensation and left us. I slumped back in an easy chair and dozed off fitfully.

Couple hours later, a nurse peeked in and turned up the pitocin drip. I stirred at this activity and pried my eyes open from disturbing obstetric dreams. "Is it working?" I asked Cheryl.

"Maybe just a little bit."

"I'm *so* tired," I said, yawning.

"Why don't you get in this bed?" she asked. "And take a nap."

"I don't think they'd like that."

"It's okay." She swung her feet onto the floor. "You climb in here, I'll sit in your chair and do this knitting."

And so, a couple hours later, my wife's obstetrician checked in to see me crashed out on the labor room bed and Cheryl purling busily in the chair provided for husbands or labor coaches. He was not happy to see it. "Just a minute," he said. "Who's having this baby?"

"Sorry," I said, waking quickly. "I was up most of the night. We have a flock of sheep. And they've just started lambing."

"Get out of that bed," he told me, shaking his head and pointing. "Cheryl—you lie down, now."

We did as we were told. He examined my wife's cervix and monitored a few contractions. No big deal yet. And then he went to the pitocin-drip machine and, I imagine, turned the dial *way* up. Enough was enough, already. Then he ducked out. Soon, Cheryl was putting down her yarn and needles.

"Getting somewhere?"

She sucked in her breath, and I counted seconds. Yes, she was getting somewhere.

Twenty minutes later, the doctor stuck his head back in. He was pleased to see his patient had lost interest in her knitting. He checked her—maybe one more hour, he determined. Then he and I stood making small talk. He had grown up on a sheep farm, too, of all things. He knew all about mummified lambs and sheep obstetrics. We swapped lies for ten minutes—no longer—when I realized that Cheryl was not following our conversation. Not in the slightest.

"Maybe you should check her," I suggested.

"I just *did* that."

"Maybe it's time to move her to the delivery room."

"I don't see how—wait a minute." Something now alerted him, something he saw that I didn't. Like the crowning of a head.

Cheryl finished her contraction, took a cleansing breath, and said: "I think I'm going to have this baby right now."

"Yes," he said. "I think so, too."

Some few contractions later our daughter lay delivered into the world, kicking and bawling in fine style. Home birth, sort of: we were still several doors down from the room with bright lights, gleaming stirrups and a tray of forceps. The pitocin-drip machine whirred softly in the background.

"So what's her name?" the doctor asked.

"*Anaïs.*"

"Very pretty."

When I drove home, some hours later, I found one more newborn wobbling to its feet in the darkened, chilly barn. A ewe lamb. *Anaïs,* I called her, and determined we would keep her in the breeding flock when she grew up.

Now—some ten years later—the ewe named Anaïs has gone the way of all old sheep, after having been a mother many times over; the child Anaïs is in fifth grade. And the mother of the child has stuck with this shepherd through an orgy of ingenious, high-tech schemes to structure ovine labor…schemes from which we've graduated back to what is natural. Still, an occasional ewe at lambing time requires a hormone boost to get her body down to business. When she has to give the shot, Cheryl does so with a grimace of keen recollection. "Listen," she will whisper, pushing the plunger on a needle buried deep into a tired ewe's hip. "Your little baby's coming *out*!"

Pumping Lambs

A few years after Anaïs's impressive birth, I got the bright idea to fool around with steroid drugs when it came time for our flock of sheep to bear their young. Many folks associate steroids with bodybuilders who will stop at nothing to add another ounce of triceps; in the sheep biz, though, I first encountered their use for a wholly different purpose. Steroids, as I came to know them, constituted a sort of last-ditch therapy for burned-out sheep. A Lazarus cure.

An older ewe in our flock had been dying—slowly, palpably—of several serious ovine complaints, and she had reached the stage where she was down and just too weak to get back up. I considered this individual a lost cause, but a visiting fellow shepherd looked the situation over and recommended a shot of dexamethasone.

"Where do I get that?" I asked. "Down at some local gym?"

"Heck, no—your vet should have it."

We drove to my vet's and bought a 100-cc. bottle of steroid for a paltry sum. Back in the barn, my colleague hit the ewe up with a modest shot of this colorless, viscous potion. I stood watching, doubtful. Not five minutes later, the old girl climbed to her feet with firm resolve. This resolution grew into unabashed alacrity, and soon she was looking for the nearest Nautilus machine.

"That's some drug!" I said.

He agreed with me. "When it works, there's no mistaking. They just sort of pick up their beds and walk."

"And when it doesn't work?"

"They roll over and die." He shrugged. "Leastways, it seems to help them make up their minds. Whether to fish or cut bait, you understand?"

I understood—and I was grateful that, in this instance, my sheep had made the more productive and convenient choice. For thirty cents—no more—we had turned around what seemed to be a terminal situation.

He handed me the scarcely tapped vial of steroid. "Some people use this to induce labor, too," he told me. "Like in case a ewe goes way past term and won't lamb on her own."

"You mean you can give this to a pregnant ewe, and she'll get busy?"

"So I've heard."

This, to me, was food for thought. In the next few weeks and months, I scoured my library of shepherding materials and quizzed several vets about the uses of this wonder drug. I even spent a night in someone else's barn, experimenting. The information I turned up was hardly scientific, but there was no question that dexamethasone had *sometimes* proved effective in inducing ewes to lamb. Results were inconsistent, though. There was disagreement on exactly what dose to give, and many times there was no response to any dose at all. On the whole, the drug worked unreliably to induce labor...except on ewes whose pregnancies were virtually at term. And how useful was *that*?

Not too many months later, the signal honor of my agrarian life occurred: I was awarded a gray ceramic bean pot emblazoned with the legend *1984 Vermont Master Lamb Producer*. This is a prize which very few, perhaps, aspire to, but which is nonetheless extremely difficult to win. In making my acceptance speech—before Vermont's Commissioner of Agriculture and a small crowd of congratulatory shepherds—I suggested that I felt we all were working much too hard for rather meager profits. My personal goal, I told them, was to find ways to spend many fewer hours with my sheep in future years without depressing their production. I exhorted my colleagues to work smarter, as I planned to do.

Basking in the glow of self-importance and accomplishment, I came to feel that a Vermont Master Lamb Producer ought to set forth an example to rank-and-file shepherds, by being unafraid to take calculated risks at innovative management of his flock. And, since spring lambing season is the chief black hole into which shepherds pour countless hours of inefficiently utilized labor—attempting to offer round-the-clock, on-call obstetric services over a four-to-six-week period—I vowed to attack the random character of parturition with unprecedented cunning. And with muscle-building drugs.

There are, it must be noted, several well-known methods for synchronizing estrus cycles in a flock of sheep so that they all get ovulating simultaneously. Come autumn of my reign as Vermont's Master Lamb Producer, I chose a simple hormone regime to accomplish this goal in forty of my ewes. A nice test group, I figured. With some effort, I provided enough ram power to see this sub-flock bred within the demanding time frame posed by simultaneous ovulation; then I segregated them to manage as a discrete group right up until lambing time. *Synchronized* lambing time.

Normal gestation in sheep can vary from 141 to 155 days, so the mere synchronization of breeding dates for forty ewes could not be expected to result in a tight lambing pattern. My plan, though, was to use dexamethasone to induce every ewe that had not lambed by day 144. Such a schedule would rule out any lamb's being born danger-ously premature but would still lop nearly ten days off the time one might expect to spend on that group's lambing chores.

April 5th worked out to be the target date for breaking out the labor-saving pharmaceutical. On April 3rd, however, I was suddenly called to Chicago in connection with a family emergency. No trouble, I told Cheryl; if I even had to come home late by a day or two, no more than half a dozen ewes in the special group might bear their lambs spontaneously. We'd still be able to trigger the majority.

With great confidence, then—and with a nagging head cold—I flew to the Midwest. I remember feeling an uncanny sense of power over nature's ways, placing a thousand miles between me and my pregnant charges without losing control over their reproductive destinies. The nature of my journey, though, cost me a lot of sleep. My cold symptoms worsened.

I was able to reserve a return flight on April 6th, but a late-season blizzard closed the airport in Vermont that day. I checked in with Cheryl. "Four lambs, last night," she reported. "Can't you get here somehow?"

"Not until tuh-murrow."

"You sound sick."

"Stuffy nose," I told her.

"Well, get back here soon. I'll make some chicken soup."

I got booked on a flight the evening of the 7th, but its takeoff from O'Hare was delayed by several hours. Sometime after two a.m., the plane landed in Vermont and I went to find my pickup buried under several feet of powdery snow. After digging it out—becoming very cold and wet in the process—I drove home. It was well past three. I changed my clothes and headed for the barn; there were *many* new lambs. Mainly, though, there were many ewes in a state of extreme and simultaneous pregnancy. They looked about ready to pop at the least suggestion. I opened a box of hypodermic needles and set to work; by sunup, I had induced thirty-four ewes with dexamethasone.

I now had an ear-splitting headache, I remember. But I also had a feeling reminiscent of what it was like to take LSD some twenty years earlier, as an incautious college student. I felt at once frightened and exhilarated: I had set in motion an irrevocable obstetric *trip,* and I mentally prepared myself to manage its challenging consequences over the next twenty-four to thirty-six hours. I went to the house and woke Cheryl to say I was home—and that we were finally rolling, so to speak.

"How's your cold?" she asked me.

"Not too good. You got a couple aspirin?"

She fixed me up and I made coffee, then fed the flock, and checked out the barn. Lo and behold, one ewe had lambed already and another one was working hard. Everyone looked great: busy, ambitious, high. The steroid was going to work like a charm. I helped the newborns dry off under heat lamps, make friends with their moms, and get their little stomachs filled with thick colostrum milk. Clean, efficient shepherding—and all around me expectant ewes were pawing the bedding, making nests, and practicing their breathing. If bodybuilders

count on steroids to help pump more iron, I thought, why, these woolly girls look ready to pump lambs. Then I felt a sudden, vast burden of fatigue; I went up to the house and told Cheryl I felt a little sick.

"*How* sick?"

"I think I might be getting a fever, even."

She kissed my forehead, then went to dig out a thermometer. Two minutes later I withdrew it from my mouth and learned how sick I was. One hundred and two, and climbing.

"Tell you what," I said. "I'll just take a little nap and then wake up at lunchtime. You and the kids can keep an eye on the barn in the meanwhile, huh?"

"What do you *mean*, keep an eye on the barn? With thirty-four ewes you just drugged to all lamb at once?"

"Sorry," I said. "Now's the best time for a nap. If things get busy down there, you can wake me."

"Right."

I crawled into bed, feeling much worse by the minute. Fact is, I was in the first feverish throes of an acute sinus infection which took several weeks to fully shake. Fact is, once I shut my eyes I managed to more or less sleep for twenty-seven hours. Not that efforts were not made to rouse me, initially. But I woke in states of increasing delirium, and after awhile there seemed little point in bothering me. There was too much action in the barn to pay me much attention.

When I rejoined the living—midday of April 9th—I staggered to the barn and beheld seventy-one new lambs. Twins, triplets, even the odd set of quads all trying to nurse madly and flexing what struck me as exceptionally well-toned muscles. There were just a few ewes left to go, and Cheryl had her arm in one of them up to her elbow, sorting out some inauspicious presentation or another while Anaïs watched. At first, I hardly recognized this good woman: hair bedraggled, eyes half shut, body zippered up into a snowmobile suit that reeked of amniotic fluid. She was in a feisty mood, though. "Golly gee!" Cheryl exclaimed. "If it's not Vermont's Master Lamb Producer!"

"I know what you're thinking," I said.

"Do you?"

"Guess I overslept." I shrugged. "I feel much better, now. Well rested."

She made a funny, high-pitched laughing sound. "I've been thinking, 'Gee whiz! Better living through chemistry! Work smart! Cut your lambing chores through more efficient use of labor!'"

"Anything else?"

"You bet. I've been thinking maybe *you* could use a little shot of steroid."

"Me? But—I'm not pregnant. Obviously."

"Lazarus therapy, remember? Fish or cut bait?"

"But—that dexamethasone's a veterinary package. Not for human use."

"I didn't think of you as human, for a while last night."

"You did good work here, though." I gestured to the scores of newborns. "In a few years, once we have this system down, you'll look back on this and—"

"Oh, no. Never again. Only way I'll ever lamb again with you is if it's laissez-faire."

Once Cheryl decides what ought to happen, I have learned not to stand in its way. The year of Pumping Lambs marked the high-water line in my career as an aggressive, modern, cutting-edge shepherd; since then, our flock management has become so laid-back that laissez-faire may be too generous a term.

And then, quite inevitably, came the year of jump-starts.

Jump-Starts

Perhaps the most depressing mistake an experienced shepherd can make is to allow significant numbers of his flock to get bred in the wrong season. I made this mistake, somehow, just four years ago. Excuses at this late date are probably beside the point, but—since my lady-sheep were perfectly modest and my boy-sheep were discreet—I might have wished some brash Iago had burst in to dash my midsummer complacency by shouting:

> *Even now, now, very now, an old black ram*
> *Is tupping your white ewe. Arise, arise!*

In Shakespeare, Othello's randy instincts were conveniently focused on a single damsel, the fair Desdemona. But sheep are not so fussy, and in retrospect I had a pair of loose cannons firing the odd shot into any of eighty potential volunteers for nearly five weeks—at a time of year when, by all accounts, fertility in sheep like mine is held to be at low ebb. I did not arise; in fact, I scarcely had a clue that any funny business had gone on till five months later—at Thanksgiving, roughly—when woolly little bundles of joy began to hit the frozen ground. Surprise, surprise! But unexpected lambs are forced to start their lives with at least two strikes against them, compared with those wiser offspring who show up consistent with their shepherd's Flock Management Plan. Then, too, some early lambs quickly collect the third strike, forfeiting their chances for higher education.

In my somewhat laid-back Flock Management Plan, ewes are scheduled to be bred during the last two weeks of each October; this gives them an excellent opportunity to drop their lambs during spring vacation of the academic calendar at Middlebury College, where a part-time teaching job has given me cause to reread Shakespeare. October breeding, too, tends to find ewes at the peak of their annual libido cycle—which means that they all ought to be ovulating earnestly, standing boldly to be mounted and eager to gestate twins.

In contrast to the sexual efficiency of autumn, for much of the usual Vermont spring and summer one does not expect a working-class ewe to even feel in the mood, much less contrive to go through estrus. As with deer and several other grazing mammals, such seasonal breeding habits represent a cunning adaptation to our northern climate: they guarantee that lactating mothers will have access to the lush, high-protein forage of early spring to help them nurse their newborn babes.

Since I don't expect my ewes to stand for any pestering, then, in July—and since it is always easier and cheaper to have livestock grazing on pasture than to feed them in the barn—I generally allow my two rams to run with their consorts until August 1. Then I hustle the big men into the barn, where they stay cool and eat grain for several weeks to boost their sperm counts. So long as the rams refrain from breaking out and following their noses to the harem, these simple measures should amount to reasonable birth control. I record the autumn day on which the rams rejoin the flock; 146 days later, I expect a shower of lambs.

I was highly disconcerted, therefore, to find a pair of lambs one chilly morn in late November, just a couple years ago. The ewes were grazing late-season, junk-food pasture in a temporary paddock half a mile from the barn; I had driven the pickup truck out with salt and water, only to find two half-licked popsicles lying on the ground. Frozen—well, one was frozen while the other was fast lapsing into hypothermic coma. I shook my head—in sorrow, sure, but also in near-disbelief. The lambs were not, apparently, premature; but lambs born in late November must have somehow been conceived around the Fourth of July! Well, it had been an extremely cool, wet summer. Possibly the weather had screwed up the internal clocks of one or two ewes, causing them to mistake Independence Day for Halloween.

I found the nonplussed mother—her flanks were brightly painted with placental fluids—and checked her milk supply, which was virtually nonexistent. No surprise: my sheep were grazing dormant vetch and various dead weeds, at the nadir of their annual nutritional cycle prior to the start of winter feeding in the barnyard. Like any thrifty shepherd, I try to keep the flock grazing until snow cover, squeezing the last nickel's worth of forage from my pastures. But late-gestation represents a crucial time for superior nutrition; malnourished fetuses lack sturdiness at birth, and udders will not swell with milk on limp, pale, frozen forage.

With growing dismay, I realized I was probably in big trouble. I wrapped my jacket round the lamb that still had chilly vital signs, propped it on the truck seat, and climbed in to chauffeur it up to the house. Then, slipping out the clutch, I eyed the flock and asked out loud: "All right—how many *more* of you ladies are on-deck?"

There are many ways to "jump-start" a chilled but living lamb: tepid baths, dextrose injections, even artificial respiration. Modern practice, though, is usually to treat the creature like a car whose gas tank has been run completely empty. Experienced drivers, faced with this dilemma, tear off the air cleaner and pour a little gasoline directly down the carburetor; shepherds likewise try to fill a lamb's stomach with warm milk. Since lambs chill down from the outside in, there's a certain rough logic to warming them up from the inside out. And even when a newborn's skin feels cold to the touch, its vital inner organs may retain enough heat to allow metabolization of energy—to burn gasoline, as combustion-minded shepherds see it. Insofar as lambs are engines, milk is their high-octane fuel.

Unfortunately, a truly chilled lamb is always much too weak to suck. And milk dribbled into one side of its mouth is apt to dribble right out the other side—or, worse, to drip into the trachea and run down into the lungs. The former route will never help revive a lamb, and the latter route can quickly kill one. So the canny shepherd feeds a catheter tube down the lamb's throat, invoking luck and talent to thread the esophageal opening rather than the trachea. Once this rubber conduit has arrived in the stomach, the free end is attached to a reservoir of warm milk; the lamb is then involuntarily fed. After the tube has been snaked out, the patient is allowed to snooze by the woodstove for half an hour or so, while its body considers whether to live or die. If it makes the animated choice, the lamb will suddenly wobble to its feet and bleat to ask, "Where's Mom?"—just as though no life-threatening episode had taken place.

Ethan and Anaïs watched, deadpan, while I catheterized my lamb on the kitchen floor and gave it a hot meal. Then, while it lay concerned with existential matters, I dug out my Flock Management notebook and was discouraged to learn I had delayed pulling out the rams till August 8 that year. On account of sheer, basic, middle-aged sloth. Staring at the calendar, I figured we were entering a five-week window of opportunity during which unwanted lambs might be born at any time. "Cheryl?" I called to my wife. "I think we'd better drive the flock into the barn and check who else is due."

"Today?" she asked the Flock Manager. "Right this morning?"

"I didn't schedule any lambs till March, but—we seem to be sitting on a time bomb, here."

"Who *did* schedule lambs for late November?"

"Just crazy weather patterns, I suppose. Erratic climate. *Mother Nature*, pulling off a fast one."

"Well," she said, "I hope you find a way to fire back."

The chilled lamb stirred, then lifted its head off the hearth and bleated in assent.

By noon, we had identified twenty-seven ewes whose udders suggested an advanced state of pregnancy. Penning these unlucky hopefuls in the barn, we marched the rest back outdoors to keep them from enjoying the sustained Thanksgiving feast I started laying on the moms-to-be: an endless buffet of second-cut hay and occasional happy hours of

whole shelled corn dusted with soybean meal for a protein wallop. I wanted to get those ewes producing milk, and pronto. As for the survivor of the lead-off set of twins, we returned it to its mother and supplemented her erratic, stunted milk supply with bottles till she improved.

Over the next two weeks, a couple dozen lambs were born and most of them had to be offered artificial milk because their moms were insufficiently primed to start lactation. These supplemental feedings were most often given via bottle, not by rubber tube; healthy newborns love to suck, and it is very hard to thread a catheter into the stomach of a squirming lamb. Catheters are not much good until a lamb is on death's doorstep. In fairness, though, we had our share of these unhappy customers, too.

On the supply side, my vet suggested tiny shots of oxytocin to help new moms let down whatever milk they had. While this hormone could do nothing to support lactation, it did work startlingly to goose up the quality of a ewe's *affection* for her hungry newborns. This was not inconsequential. Love-in-a-bottle, we came to call that vial of colorless injectable. Armed, then, with syringes and catheters and nipples, we fought back bravely against nature's capriciousness in gifting us with far too many unexpected lambs. If their engines wanted to sputter and die, well, we had ways to make them idle properly. Like it or not. Just like fiddling with the choke on a reluctant engine.

The strangest phenomenon began to occur, however: lambs whose first experience of milk came from a bottle—held horizontal, with the precious liquid dribbling freely from a rubber nipple—tended not to make a satisfactory transition to their own mothers' flesh-and-blood teats even after hormonal and dietary therapy had made fresh milk available. At first, the kids would call these babies *too dumb to suck*—and then we began to call them many other things, as well, after tortuously arranging their mouths around their mothers' teats only to have them steadfastly refuse to nurse. It was as though having the first-meal experience from a latex nipple spoiled the lambs' appreciation of the real thing. Here was an anomaly: in our efforts to keep newborn lambs alive, we were producing lambs too screwed-up to survive without us.

Voicing this complaint to a wiser shepherd than myself, I learned about a special tool called an *esophageal probe*, obtainable from a Nebraska veterinarian named Joseph Magrath. A long-distance phone call to the doctor's warehouse had one coming to me, air-express; the gadget arrived a couple days later, and by Christmas this Magrath Probe had saved me more lambs than I care to tally.

The lamb-size esophageal probe consists of an eight-inch stainless-steel tube with flared base and adaptive clamp to screw onto the business end of any large syringe; the tip of the probe is a teardrop-shaped casting whose engineered size and shape prohibits it from entering a baby lamb's trachea at the crucial junction where windpipe and gullet merge. Unlike working with a catheter tube, with Magrath's Probe one can't make the truly awkward mistake of depositing a stomach feeding smack into a newborn's lungs and drowning the patient right before one's eyes.

Sliding the esophageal probe down a lamb's throat, one feels brief resistance at the epiglottal flap; then, a moment later, one is all the way into the stomach. Bingo! And because the probe is perfectly rigid, a properly positioned lamb need not be half-dead to receive its ministrations. Best of all, the probe does not contaminate a newborn's latent sense of what a real teat should look like—or feel like, or operate like—when and if the lamb eventually has the joy of finding one. Repeated meals via Magrath's Probe may well produce a wicked sore throat, but a lamb's vital suckling instinct runs no risk of lasting damage.

And so Joseph Magrath got us out of quite a jam that winter. Until our crash nutrition program brought some milk into the ewes, each newborn got a squirt of milk at birth to start its motor. Just like dripping gasoline into an engine's carburetor. Usually, this unsought meal caused a lamb to want to lie down for a little nap, and by the time it woke we'd have the mom as eager to be suckled as hormones could make her. Nursing can mechanically stimulate lactation, too—even when an udder doesn't have a lot of milk to start with.

I don't claim that we pulled all those early-winter lambs through, and I'd hate ever to live through such a month again. Untimely, unexpected breeding has its costs—no question. But, to an astonishing extent, we succeeded in forcing inauspicious lambs to live, and causing too-thin ewes to lactate. Possible moral, then: when nature tosses one a curve, unnatural measures may be needed to regain control. Or perhaps it's much more simple. One just needs an inner voice—even in July—to shout: "Arise, arise! It's midnight, dummy! Do you know where your rams are?"

End of the Road

There are only three ways to improve the average quality of animals in a livestock enterprise, and one of them—buying better blood—can be terribly expensive, quite aside from the risks of bringing in disease. The other two ways are to save the offspring of identified superior animals in the herd and to get rid of identified losers. This latter procedure is called *culling*. On a well-tuned farm, each breeding animal's performance is reviewed at least annually, and any culls are speedily removed.

Our farm has become, in several gross-management respects, less and less well tuned with each passing year; I blame middle age and a centripetal scattering of energy which, to the untrained eye, is easily confused with laziness. When I was an astute farm manager, I culled any female sheep who had failed to bear twin lambs for me by the age of eighteen months. Those intensive days are gone, though. A few winters ago, I looked up one morning from competing concerns to note that out of the eighty ewes I fed each day, there were certainly a few whose reproductive efforts failed to justify their feed costs.

As with so many of life's thorny problems, economics played a role in my lackadaisical approach to culling chores. In 1983, for example, the nearest terminal market that I knew would purchase old, tired, worn-out sheep was 200 miles away, and a cull sheep taken there would bring about seven cents per pound on the hoof—or about ten dollars. Trucking costs alone could gobble up that paltry sum and place my culling efforts in a net debit situation. So it proved less painful to let old, postmenopausal ewes wander about with the rest of the flock until they dropped of natural causes.

This entropic situation might have gone on forever, but like so many other Americans, I was on the verge of acquiring a personal computer. We took the plunge in 1985, for no particularly compelling reason. After processing the odd word or two, I pondered what other nifty tricks I could make this tool do. Lo and behold, I turned up complicated software written expressly to help modern shepherds keep watch over their flocks. I obtained one of these sheep production programs and, in the course of several chilly winter evenings, transferred such records as I had about each sheep onto a floppy disk. And then I asked the wise machine: Which are the really good ewes in this flock of sheep? And which are the bad ones?

The computer program enabled me to ask these questions in a surprisingly sophisticated fashion. I entered the weights of every ewe's lambs at weaning time and factored in the value of each ewe's yearly fleece. Then I persuaded the machine to express each ewe's production as a percentage of the *average* ewe's production in the flock. In a flash, the computer spat out the ear-tag numbers of sheep who were producing at 140% of the flock average. Super-ewes. Then, too, certain sheep were called to my attention who were producing barely 40% of the flock average. Or less. One or two sheep, in fact, were scarcely producing anything at all.

Having this intelligence firmly in hand would have caused me nothing but chagrin, were it not for the fact that I had heard about a livestock auction held each Monday afternoon on the far side of Vermont. Two mountain ranges and one hundred miles away—but not all that far, as these things go. Unlike any of the local livestock auctions, this one had developed a competitive market for animals other than Holstein cattle. A fellow could fill his pickup truck with cull ewes, drive a couple of hours, and fully expect to sell them for more money than he had just forked out in gasoline.

I took my computer printout to the barn and sorted sheep. The computer had, with incredible ease, identified the ear-tag numbers of my culls; but I now found that many sheep had *removed* their ear tags over the course of time—or removed each other's ear tags in a stroke of cunning sociability. It is well and good to know that ewe G234, say, is a dog of a sheep and a drag on the flock average. But which of fifteen ewes, none of which has kept her ear tag, *is* she? I couldn't help reminiscing that there was a time when I could attach a name to every sheep's *face*. Small flock. Large losses, though. With something less than Solomonic justice, I picked through the tag-less pen for any sheep about which there was something I didn't like. And then I got the truck loaded.

I invited Ethan and Anaïs to come with me to the auction. "Too busy," said the fifth grader. "Boring," said his preschool sister. But I kept at them, characterizing the journey as a rural analog to visiting the zoo. This proved, in fact, to be surprisingly accurate. Soon the three of us were roaring over snowy mountains, singing together and swapping stories.

"I think one of those sheep just jumped out of the truck," Ethan told me soberly.

"Impossible," I said, hitting the brakes.

"How many were there?"

"Nine."

"Let me count," offered Anaïs. Since she was just learning to count, it took a long time. But it turned out there were nine.

"Well, one *could* jump out," my son said.

"Maybe. But sheep usually stick together." Some of those sheep, it occurred to me, had been sticking together for nearly a decade. And in all that time, this was their first ride in a truck. Virtually their last one, too, since ewes of a certain age are good only for sausage. I did not disguise this from my children, but neither one was at an age where such news caused alarm. They were merely curious to see who might buy our old sheep. I was curious, myself.

The East Thetford Commission Sale occupied a sprawling, down-at-the-heels barn in a town so small that it dominated what passed for a business district. I backed the pickup to a sliding door, and a stout young woman started poking metal tags, called hog rings, into each sheep's ear. She did this with special pliers and an unflinching grip. An older man then wrote down the tag numbers in a tattered notebook; when I volunteered my name and address, he wrote those down, too, in a barely legible scrawl.

"No receipt?" I asked politely.

"Nuh."

"But—"

"Got your name right here."

I thought of the computer age which I was stumbling into, and

I looked at his weathered spiral notebook as though it were some rude abacus. And then I shrugged: when in Rome. I opened up the truck bed, chased the sheep into the barn, and helped the man and woman herd them into a holding pen. Then I took the kids to wander a maze of dimly lit corridors in search of the auction ring.

By and large, the barn was full of very young and very old creatures waiting to be sold. There were just-weaned piglets, scarcely bigger than a football; there were day-old male calves who wobbled on their feet and whose umbilical cords were still thick and bloody. There were pens of goats and ponies, hens and turkeys, ducks and rabbits. And there were old dairy cows of every size and type and breed.

After making a thoughtful tour of this menagerie, we opened a wooden door that led into the auction. The room was hot and packed and smoke-filled. Several dozen dour, taciturn farmers and steely-eyed meat buyers were seated on rough bleachers that surrounded three sides of a twelve-by-twelve-foot ring; on the fourth side, an auctioneer and book-keeper ran the show from a raised dais. As I pushed my kids toward upper seats, the ringman led in a huge, wild horse and tapped its buttocks with a cane.

"All right, boys. You see him. Eight years old, and he ain't broken yet. So take him home and you can break him any way you like!"

The crusty faces broke into crinkles of laughter, and a farmer just in front of me told his neighbor: "That horse ain't nothing but a big pile of hamburger. That's all he is."

His neighbor nodded in agreement. "You ever eat any of that hamburger from an old, unbroken horse?" he asked. "I tell you. If you're chewing, and somebody hollers 'Whoa!,' you're like to choke to death!"

The horse sold for one hundred and fifteen dollars, which was cheap hamburger indeed. Then a one-eyed pony was led in. On a rope lead, he began to race around the pen.

"Okay, boys. You see it. Only one eye, but I swear he sees enough with just that one, by God. Start it off at forty dollars. Forty? Well, then, thirty-five."

"Wouldn't you like to have that pony?" an old farmer asked my wide-eyed daughter.

"No," she said. "I wouldn't."

The pony, who never ceased trotting in circles round the tiny ring, was sold a few minutes later for forty-one dollars.

Cattle were led in and sold, beginning with the day-old calves and working up through vealers, springing heifers, and tired old cows. On high-ticket items—a couple of the heifers fetched around four hundred dollars—the auctioneer would force the bidding in five-dollar increments till he smelled the finish line. Then he would drop to one-dollar increments—or less—until he found his buyer. When his hammer hit the stand, everybody knew *exactly* what an animal was worth.

Finally, our ewes were led in. They bunched up together, bashful and confused, and the auctioneer barked: "You lookit here, boys. Good sheep. *Good* sheep. Now, there's nothing wrong with these here ewes except for their age."

"AIDS?" asked the ringman coyly.

"Age."

"Do these sheep have AIDS?"

All the thin-lipped farmers creased the corners of their mouths again, and the auctioneer explained my sheep did not have AIDS but age. Old sheep. In damned good flesh, though. Start the bidding off at thirty bucks a head, and the winner could take his pick.

Two meat buyers divided the lot, at prices ranging from twenty-five to forty dollars per head. After commissions and gasoline, I was looking at a couple hundred dollars for nine culls. With considerable pleasure, I packed the kids back into the truck and drove them home.

Two days later—sure enough—my check came in the mail. It was written in the same rough scrawl as the auction's sign-in book, and it was for a considerably larger sum than I was owed. Deciphering the stub, I saw that I was being paid for several Holstein calves as well as for my sheep. But this was not my fault, I figured. I ran the check past the bank, entered the receipts in my computerized financial records, and kept my mouth shut.

Couple days later, another handwritten receipt came in the mail. "You owe us," it said. "Please send check. Sorry for the error." And there was some fine print at the bottom of the form: ALL STOCK LEFT AT OWNER'S RISK. WE ACT AS AGENTS ONLY. SUBJECT TO CORRECTION OF CLERICAL ERRORS.

My computer keeps much better track of these details, and yet, I thought, reaching for my checkbook—my computer doesn't sell cull sheep. And I might have a few to sell again, someday.

Infection vs. Incest

A friend of mine recently visited the Amazon to study the rain forest's ongoing demise. He brought a nagging, Yanqui-style head cold with him, and one morning when he entered an isolated jungle village, he sneezed once or twice. Almost immediately, fifty natives had red eyes, swollen glands, and runny noses; they had absolutely no previous experience with whatever bug he had carried into their midst. When he returned home, he, too, exhibited unusual symptoms that did not fit any simple diagnosis. When discrete cultures are allowed to interact, infection is predictably a two-way street.

Something like that happens on a sheep farm, too, when new animals from outside are introduced into a flock. The fresh breeding stock may appear perfectly sound and healthy; otherwise, why would a smart shepherd have purchased them? And one's own ewes may have been infection-free for months or even years. But when they are mixed together, all too often the result is an epidemic of coughing, or pink eye, or some far worse sickness. Subclinical maladies suddenly go public, and the veterinary cost of getting on top of things may leave a shepherd feeling rather ill, too.

The one sure way to avoid this kind of grief is to maintain a "closed" flock—like a small, isolated Amazon tribe denied any contact with the outside world. That is how I like to run our modest flock of sheep: animals routinely leave here to become somebody else's breeding stock, or—more often—to become someone's dinner, but nothing that goes *Baaa* is allowed to come back up the driveway. I used to chauffeur sheep to several shows and county fairs each year, to advertise their merits, but nowadays I wouldn't dare. They might try to make friends with some heavy breather in the next pen; after staying too long at the fair, it could take me months to mop up the consequences.

In fact, my mania for keeping the flock "closed" once caused me to throw out a perfectly good pair of shoes that I wore to the farm of a fellow shepherd. We walked out to have a look at his flock and discovered several ewes limping painfully across the pasture. Hoof rot. I had walked where they had walked; the soles of my sneakers had very likely picked up the bacteria that patiently reduce sheep's feet to fetid, dark, necrotic mush. Once hoof rot gains a toehold on a farm, full eradication is just about impossible. I wanted nothing doing. So I tossed my shoes into a trash bin at a roadside rest area and drove back to my farm unshod.

As a breeding strategy, however, keeping a flock of sheep ruthlessly closed entails patent risks. If selected progeny from a single ram are saved as replacement ewes and bred back to their fathers, and then if some of *their* daughters are bred back to their grandfather, and then if—well. Conventional wisdom holds that such inbreeding ought to produce, in time, a flock of so many hemophiliacs and idiots.

Still, six years ago I started down that road. Since more than a few of my sheep seemed pretty dumb to start with, I had no particular cause to fear idiocy; as for hemophilia, I considered it a far less serious condition than some of the diseases I might introduce into the flock by bringing in a brand-new ram every couple years. Good rams cost good money, too, and may take years to prove they can impart to their progeny the traits for which one purchased them.

When truly pressed to justify my policy of inbreeding, I liked to point out that the royal houses of Europe were also thoroughly inbred for centuries. They produced their share of hemophiliacs and idiots —true—but they also produced many leaders of unquestionable talent, even genius. The actual effect of inbreeding, I maintained, is to make recessive traits express themselves. Grow dominant. If the recessive traits inherent in a pool of genes are, on the whole, lousy, then inbreeding isn't apt to bring forth thrilling specimens. If, on the other hand, magnificent traits are hiding in the gene pool, lurking in recession, inbreeding may be the quickest, surest route to genetic progress.

In the sheep-breeding business, few of us are trying to produce leaders of genius or even sheep with exceptionally high IQs. The traits we long to see reliably manifested in each crop of lambs have to do with growth rate, feed conversion ability, and carcass quality. And then, for replacement ewes, we like to see prolificacy, mothering ability, and desirable fleece characteristics. These are the "genius" traits in the ovine world, and after a couple years of casual inbreeding I had cause to think I was improving the flock's performance in nearly all these areas.

I found out something else, too, by following this Jukes-and-Kallikaks breeding program. The "bad" traits in my flock, when allowed to express themselves, were nothing so complex as idiocy or hemophilia. They tended to be skeletal and structural deformities, and these nearly always turned out to be quickly lethal. No one likes to see a newborn lamb that can't get to its feet because a leg joint hinges in the wrong direction, but such an awkward problem quickly resolves itself: lambs that cannot stand and find a teat and suckle it are simply not long with us. I may be dismayed if one or two lambs in a hundred emerge from the womb with crippling birth defects. But that strikes me as a small price to pay to guarantee the whole flock's freedom from infectious illness.

Nothing lasts forever, though, and just a couple years ago I was forced to admit that our best ram was having libido problems. Actually, Ethan and Anaïs forced me to admit it: they ran into the house one crisp November morning, breathless, to announce that Mister Right and Ginger were having sex.

"*Ginger*?" Ginger is the 115-pound Great Pyrenees dog—a spayed bitch—who lives with our sheep to guard them from predators. "Well," I said, "it *is* toward the end of the breeding season. Maybe Mister Right has run out of ewes, and—"

"You don't understand," said Ethan. "Ginger's breeding Mister Right!"

"Oh, no. You kids must have—"

"Just come and see, if you don't believe us."

I went to the pasture with them and returned home badly shaken. Ginger was indeed mounting our prize sire—repeatedly—despite the fact that he was well over twice her size. Many farm animals use mimicry of coitus as a means of establishing rank in the pecking order, but it was absurd for my 275-pound ram to let himself be dominated by the family dog. Unless he was very nearly over the hill.

The real proof came in the following spring, when our lambs dribbled in over a seven-week period. Since the estrus cycle in sheep is only fifteen days, a highly sexed ram can theoretically cover every ewe in a flock like ours in about two weeks. Given normal variations in gestation, a tightly bunched crop of lambs can hit the ground in just three weeks—saving many sleepless nights for lambing attendants. Mister Right had done his job; we did get our lambs, in time. But plainly, he had had some trouble keeping it up during the critical first two weeks of breeding.

"This might be the year to buy a ram," Cheryl suggested wearily, one night deep in April. It was two weeks past the point when lambing season should have stopped.

"Or I might just save one from the lamb crop," I countered.

"That's not very smart, is it?"

"We could go through all our records and pick out the very best. Best lamb from the best mother—I haven't castrated any of the ram lambs yet."

"Doesn't this flock need new blood?"

"Maybe, but it's riskier with every passing year. There are sheep diseases in New England like we never had before. Imported from out West. Like scrapie—get this, the entire nervous system just slowly degenerates. Like vibriosis—hey, every other ewe in a flock aborts her lambs at term. Like—"

"Still, you can't just inbreed sheep indefinitely."

"Watch me." I dragged out the flock records and began searching for a special young man. Soon enough he jumped right out at me from the tattered pages of dry, cold statistics: R152, a triplet with the whopping birth weight of nine pounds. His mother, T16, had weaned in excess of a hundred pounds of lamb for several years running. She had never required obstetric assistance, and two of her daughters had made good as members of the flock. Even her fleece weights came in heavier than average. "Here's our boy," I told Cheryl, thumping the page. "R152. The future! We'll grow him out big and strong and get him on the job by autumn."

"You're going to let him breed his sisters? Breed his own mother?"

"Sure, if he can stomach it. I think it's all the same, for sheep. They don't have these taboos."

"I'm not *talking* about taboos," said Cheryl. "I'm talking about freaks, and—"

"Trust me. R152—come on, give the kid a chance."

A couple weeks later, I penned all the ram lambs in the barn to render them *castrati* as required by the marketing co-operative for which we raise them. I kept my eye out for R152, however, and when his turn came I just gave him a wink and an encouraging pat on the head. For an eight-week-old, he looked terrific: broad saddle, thick thighs, eager and alert. Promising little scrotal pouch, too. I named him Balzac on the spot, and lifted him to freedom with his testicles intact.

Soon enough the flock went out to pasture for the summer months, and that was the last I saw of Balzac until weaning day. He still looked great, although I remember noting that he walked with a peculiar limp. Sprain, maybe. But he was rather well grown, for a triplet, and his muscling was just superb. I gave him a worming shot and placed him on feed with his fifty half-brothers—eunuchs, every one of them—and fifty pubescent half-sisters. He quickly proved capable of living like a sultan, and I knew my ewes would have a stud in whom I could place confidence.

That puzzling limp, though. It never really went away, and I was forced to discard my theory that Balzac had suffered some minor injury. Finally—it was in November, just a week or so before I planned to let him show his stuff to the flock of ewes—I flipped my little man and examined his legs carefully. His two front ankles canted inward by a few degrees, making him just slightly pigeon-toed. So: he wasn't actually limping, after all. He just had a funny walk.

I guess I should have sat right down, slapped myself hard, and shouted: "Structural deformity!" I didn't, though. Sometimes the "hot," all-grain diet used to fatten lambs can weaken their pasterns; once returned to hay and pasture, strength returns to weakened ankles. Maybe that was Balzac's problem. Anyway, I knew it would be futile—and foolhardy, too—to go shopping for a ram just days before I needed him. Even had I chosen to shop. And, aside from this fairly minor foot problem, Balzac seemed to be a superior ram lamb in every trait that mattered.

I turned him out, a few days later, to consort with his sisters and his cousins and his aunts. And his mother, too. He demonstrated fully developed instinct, perfect aim, and an appetite for sex that can only be described as indefatigable.

We have taken to having our shearer ply his trade here just before the start of lambing season, since our barn is nearly twice as roomy once the sheep are shorn. I can still recall walking Balzac onto the shearing floor for his first fleecing and the puzzled expression on the shearer's face when he guided his tool across the ram's front shoulder. Since shearers are on fairly intimate terms with the anatomy of sheep, I was surprised to see him pause, then stop and shut down his machine. He felt beneath the wool, assessing where the shank of Balzac's arm left the shoulder-blade.

"Something wrong?" I asked him, nonchalant.

"He's *very* incorrect. You used this ram for breeding?"

"Well, I—yes. I did."

"Who sold you this ram?"

"Nobody. I bred him. Right here. This is a closed flock, understand? That's how I keep these sheep healthy."

He couldn't help a funny grin from furrowing his cheeks. "Well," he told me, "you may have an interesting lamb crop."

Balzac sired ninety-seven lambs, and half a dozen of them hit the ground with structural deformities much like his own. Cheryl made a few fairly withering remarks; in the end I accepted the blame for everything and promised we would neither keep nor sell any breeding stock out of that year's crop. Every lamb would go for slaughter. And then I agreed to buy a new ram for the coming year—fresh blood, from the outside world—and I did that, too. I quarantined the incoming stud for three months straight and then introduced him to the flock without infectious incident...yet. You never know, of course; some ovine diseases can take years to incubate, and others lie dormant till some optimal environment causes them to bloom.

But while I have not written off the disease risks one assumes by mixing sheep, I have learned there are clear and present dangers attached to a policy of incest, too. Prolonged incest, anyway. There are devils known and unknown; there is just no way to manage a population without flirting with various catastrophes. Over time—no matter whether one imports new blood or inbreeds—caring for a flock of sheep can be like blowing up a photo: sooner or later, one way or another, you are apt to get to see exactly what is hiding there.

Taking Care of Business

F arming has a way of teaching economics even to those who never learned to distinguish supply curves on the textbook graphs of price formation. Even to people like me, that is to say. After raising sheep in Vermont for just a little while, I became impressed with how difficult it can be to sell a meat-lamb in New England for anything like what it costs to raise one here. The "farm-gate" price of lamb is set quite far from *my* farm gate—in places like Texas, Colorado, and New Zealand— and there's very little that any one shepherd can do to fetch a penny more than the going market price, any given day. Sometimes I have had to sell lambs that did not even fetch *that* price, for one reason or another. Sometimes I have had to sell cheap what cost me dearly to produce.

Marketing wool can be an even more depressing story. Most sheep grow about a seven-pound fleece per year; in autumn of 1990, thanks to vagaries of worldwide supply and demand, the wholesale price of wool in Vermont was just twenty-seven cents per pound. Not even enough to pay a shearer! *Polyester* sells for more. Shepherds a hundred years ago received a better price, without adjustment for inflation.

Farmers, of course, are inveterate grousers, and nobody is forcing any of us to keep our hands on the plow. Those that linger in our game either like to lose money—perhaps as a way of ducking taxes on other income—or have learned, against all odds, how to take care of business. I count myself in the latter camp, most years. Just because our farm does not produce an income we can live on doesn't mean I manage it unprofitably. It just means the profits are tenuous and uncomfortably *slim*. On a per-hour basis, people make more money pumping gas. Cleaning houses. Flipping burgers. These facts may embarrass me and make me feel kind of silly, but they can never drive the farm into bankruptcy. I have learned to make a dollar. I know how to run this business.

Like any other business, there have been tricks galore to unearth and master on the road to profit. An ongoing partnership with agencies of government—and with generous taxpayers, too—has helped immeasurably. Marketing co-operatives have managed to stabilize the worst fluctuations in the prices of the crops we sell, as well as the various production inputs we must purchase. Learning the ins and outs of "niche" markets, such as that for breeding stock, has also served us well. The goodwill generated by giving farm tours to schoolchildren, day-care centers, and other groups has had a certain business value, not to mention the sheer joy of showing off the farm.

With passing years, our *own* schoolchildren have gotten involved with taking care of business. Fewer and fewer chores exceed their mental and physical resources, and they have a way of approaching Herculean labors with an enthusiasm I remember from my youth. Just three years ago, I thought it might be simpler and easier to build *new* sheep barns than to clean the ones I have. Now I'm not so sure. Paying kiddie wages is my fastest-growing farm expense, but hey—at least a buck or two is staying in the family.

Here, then, are some tales about learning to take care of business.

Farming the Government

In an era of widespread agricultural recession, frustrated tillers of the soil advise each other to try *farming the government*, as though the U.S. Department of Agriculture represented an alternative crop. It's a wonderfully apt phrase, meaning that each farm management decision ought to be made with a view to reaping maximum bucks from a plethora of federal programs. Compared to the fickle character of market prices for farm commodities, government checks are something of a sure thing. And they have a way of just not bouncing.

Fourteen years ago, when I first joined the ranks of Vermont shepherds, the last thing on my mind was shoving my snoot into the public trough. And, as things turned out, the government deals available for sheep producers did not hold a patch to what some others were making off with. No feds have ever offered to pay me, for example, to produce fewer pounds of lamb or wool than I am able. Feds have never urged me to accept a handsome sum of cash—as thousands of dairymen recently did—to slaughter my entire breeding flock and desist from business for five years. These folks got to farm the government, big-time. I do, however, benefit from a modest price-support program that distorts the economics of wool production. Good thing, too—else I long ago would have used genetic selection to breed sheep that would not bother growing wool at all.

In the Northeast, where real estate tends to be scarce and dear, most shepherds concentrate on lamb production because that is how the bills get paid. It's not unusual to find a good ewe weaning up to a hundred dollars' worth of lamb per year; her annual fleece, on the other hand, is apt to have a gross market value of no more than seven dollars. Or less. That's *before* paying sundry production costs, such as two to four dollars to have each sheep shorn in the first place.

This situation might have moved *me* to become a shearer; but when I tried, I found certain requisite back muscles to be sadly atrophied or nonexistent. I spent a comical afternoon inflicting myself on three or four members of my worried flock. Part of the time I was standing up and they were down; more of the time, they were standing up and I was down. Several times I nearly gave a new, unintended meaning to my stated goal of learning how to shear myself. Then, to my animals' palpable relief, I quit.

And so I hired the proverbial professional. When it came time to pay this good man the lion's share of my fleeces' paltry value, he said: "Listen—don't feel bad. You can get this money right back from the government."

"I can?"

"Sure. From the Wool Act. Just get a signed receipt when you sell your wool, and take it to the county agricultural office. Check comes in the spring, around April 15—when it ought to come in handy, right?"

I *liked* the idea of having the government pay me a little something just when I was getting squared away with the IRS. A phone call to the local office of the Agricultural Stabilization and Conservation Service—the branch of government that pays farmers to do or not do all sorts of things—proved the shearer right: the Wool Act for the year in question, 1975, had set a target price of seventy-two cents per pound of wool. Since the average market price was running more like forty-five cents, the government was gearing up to pay shepherds whatever amount of money it would take to lift the average market price to seventy-two cents. But there was a kicker, too: the same *percentage* price support would be applied to *whatever* a given producer had received for his wool.

"I don't understand," I confessed to this bureaucrat. He didn't seem a bit surprised.

"Let's say we calculate the national wool payment at sixty percent," he told me. "If you sell your wool for forty-five cents a pound, the sixty percent payment adds twenty-seven cents, bringing you up to seventy-two cents—target. But let's say you sell your wool for a buck a pound. You would still get another sixty percent from the government. So then you'd get sixty cents a pound. Bringing your total up to a dollar sixty."

"Why?"

"That's to give you an *incentive* to produce the best wool you can."

"Wow!" I said. "Now, what if I sell all this wool to my mother? For *five* bucks a pound?"

"No," he told me—but I'm sure he sensed that I was catching on. "It has to be what we call an arm's-length transaction. No obvious funny business."

"So where *do* I sell these fleeces?"

He said: "Better join a wool pool."

I spent the next few weeks investigating this advice. In the Northeast, where there are few large bands of sheep, wool is usually marketed in sales which pool the fleeces of many flocks to create sufficient volume to attract a wholesale buyer's notice. Different wool pools have differing reputations, too; since the product is typically purchased sight unseen, reputation counts for plenty. What shepherds have stuffed, at shearing time, into eight-foot burlap sacks had better be predominantly wool rather than burdocks and hay chaff and "tags" of dried manure, all of which cling to inferior fleeces. These forms of contamination can be bagged and sold as wool—once. Next time around, the buyer's bid will drop precipitously. Forty-five cents per pound is no great price for wool, but it is a very good price for manure and garbage.

In fact, I learned that shepherds like to tell "Can-you-top-this?" tales about unexpected treats tucked away in wool sacks and sold across the scales of an unsuspecting wool pool. Bricks, say. Two-by-fours. The green, unsalted hides of farm-slaughtered sheep and lambs. And—I swear I heard this story—an entire dead ewe packed into a burlap sack, carefully surrounded by the fleeces of its former mates. When a wool pool acquires a reputation for such chicanery, wholesalers steer clear altogether; on the other hand, reputable wool pools can consistently top the going market price. And then participants get doubly rewarded by the government's price support.

As a fledgling shepherd, I was fortunate to get linked with the quality-conscious wool pool run by the Vermont Sheep Breeders Association. This event, held annually in a barn owned by the Windham Foundation in Grafton, Vermont, has become an annual outing at roughly the peak of autumn foliage. Scores of far-flung shepherds converge on a riotously colorful Saturday to weigh and number several hundred sacks containing, in aggregate, up to thirty tons of wool. Then the sacks are loaded onto waiting tractor-trailers and hauled off to the buyer's woolen mill. Some weeks later, checks representing the cash sale price arrive in the mail; the following April, the government sends out its kicker.

At my first wool pool, I voiced some vague misgivings about signing up to receive this government largesse, but various fellow producers quickly set me straight. In the first place, said one, wool checks did not really come out of the taxpayers' pockets.

"No?" I asked.

"Money for the Wool Act is supposed to come from tariffs on textile imports. That way, we can meet unfair foreign competition. But Washington collects more money from that tariff than they ever pay out to shepherds. So actually, taxpayers are making money off us."

A sometime advocate of free trade, I nevertheless managed to find this argument persuasive. Simple matter of whose ox is being gored, I guess. No sooner was my guilt assuaged, when a burly, bearded man climbed out of a wool sack he was stomping around in, packing sundry fleeces, to tell me the importance of promoting the domestic product. A "check-off" system built into the Wool Act, he explained, is the chief funding vehicle for the American Sheep Producers Council, which spends millions of dollars every year touting U.S. lamb and wool to

American consumers. Not to sign up for a government check was tantamount to sabotaging our industry's great, historic mission.

"Gee," I said, "I'd hate to do a thing like that. But why does the government support wool in the first place?"

"Because," said an intense woman crouched behind a calculator at the accounting table, "wool happens to be a strategic commodity."

"*Strategic?*"

"For the military."

Now I had to laugh. "Like platinum?" I asked. "Like bauxite? Like uranium?"

"Just try to make a decent military uniform without wool."

Amazing, I thought. "You mean, without woolen uniforms our national defense would grind to a halt?"

"Do you know what happens to polyester uniforms in the heat of battle?"

"Search me."

"They can *melt*. And then soldiers become burn victims."

"Okay, okay," I said. "I'll take the price support. Sign me up."

Since I had only about sixty pounds of wool to sell, that first year, my handout from the government's Commodity Credit Corporation was for a paltry sum—not even enough to buy a decent woolen sweater. But in a few years' time, our flock had grown and so had the government's wool program, that hidden bulwark of national defense. At its peak, the government once paid me five hundred dollars to help me get over selling five hundred pounds of wool for only three hundred dollars in the marts of trade. And I got darn near five hundred dollars more to thank me for growing the wool on the hides of unshorn lambs I sold for slaughter— wool that would have been completely uneconomic to shear off their backs in the first place.

Those days are over, though. Wool price supports have been scaled back substantially; slowly but steadily, shepherds are being weaned off the federal teat. Last year's wool receipts—including that nifty check from the government—were not enough to pay my shearer. How long, in such circumstances, will Americans grow wool? Still, I have appreciated my ongoing pittance from the federal treasury. I would be worse off without it. Somebody, somewhere, surely must be getting fleeced, but I have enjoyed helping our soldiers dress in spiffy style. Fact is, anytime I see someone in uniform, I want to salute.

Meatman

Unlike most farmers, I toiled for many years without having a marketing co-operative to kick around. Co-ops in agriculture give farmers the legal right to collude in setting prices, since otherwise they would be atomized sellers in a marketplace dominated by relatively few hard-nosed buyers. After farmers have spent many months or years to grow a perishable crop, they are at risk of getting robbed when monopolistic wholesalers dictate the crop's value. Take it or leave it, Jack. Co-ops redress this imbalance of power by allowing farmers to gang up and sell their goods collectively.

The big co-ops—those for dairy farmers, say, or wheat producers—have grown very big indeed. They own extensive processing and storage facilities. They have bulging payrolls. Most farmers could scarcely do business without their co-ops, but many can be heard to mutter about them in the same breath with the federal bureaucracy, the telephone company, and similar institutional octopi. For every paean to the ideal of co-operation, there are half a dozen loud complaints of getting screwed.

I used to feel left out in farmers' conversations when the subject turned to co-ops; several years ago, though, I became a founding member of Yankee Shepherd, Inc., a lamb-marketing concern with ambitious plans and almost nonexistent assets. The thirty-odd original members were raising several thousand lambs each year, sufficient volume to enable hiring a manager to woo upscale markets and offer them meat that had a special cachet.

The concept underlying Yankee Shepherd owed a lot to Frank Perdue: by offering labeled, name-branded lamb products, producers hoped to command premium prices in a market dominated by generic meat. Initially, a key label was simply "Vermont Lamb," identified by a carcass stamp akin to those used by meat inspectors. Vermont Lamb would have the word VERMONT stamped all over it, and jealous imitators would not be allowed to use the stamp. In gourmet meat cases, in food-service channels, and on the menus of various expensive restaurants, Vermont Lamb was supposed to catch on as a five-star treat.

Yankee Shepherd quickly thrived, after a fashion. By 1984, up to a hundred lambs per week were being hawked at prices generally higher than national wholesale markets paid. The future seemed bright. And then—to make things brighter still—the co-op's manager was asked to go to Montreal and huddle with some bureaucrats about funneling many thousands of lambs from New England into Quebec. Top-of-the-market pricing. Monster volume. Easy money.

The manager asked me to drive his delivery route while he went to Montreal for the lamb powwow. Sure, I said. In part, I have a weakness for the spirit of co-operation; but I have a greater weakness for offbeat experiences. And so, crack of dawn on a muddy April morn, he left the Yankee Shepherd truck in my rutted driveway and handed over a clipboard of instructions.

Back in those early days, the Yankee Shepherd truck did not belong to Yankee Shepherd. It was the manager's own aging pickup, fitted with a slide-in cooler that the co-op's directors had bought second-hand. This single corporate asset had not cost a lot, and looked it. DAIRY TESTING—MILK SAMPLES read the faded paint on one side of the box. Its rear door had a way of not latching, sometimes. Its reefer, or refrigeration unit, ran off the truck's engine through a complicated series of controls, each of which had a mind of its own. All things considered, the truck provided small improvement over delivering meat out of a station wagon. It also projected a corporate image of erstwhile destitution.

First stop for me was the nearest gas station, where I boldly asked an attendant to fill her up. This took quite some time and a lot of money, because the manager had added a second twenty-gallon tank to the truck's original reservoir of fuel. When hauling meat, which absolutely *must* stay refrigerated, running out of gas can be the worst sort of catastrophe. Some fifty dollars later, I aimed the creaking pickup toward the nearest interstate and headed for a slaughterhouse sixty miles away.

At R&E Meats, Inc., several dozen co-op lambs hung side by side in a cavernous cooler. Overhead, a maze of rails snaked along the ceiling like an inverted switchyard for the hooks that held our meat. I began stamping VERMONT on the hard white fat that covered the carcasses' backs and buttocks; then an R&E worker helped me pull a long, clear plastic bag over each lamb. Next, we rolled each carcass along the overhead track to a scale where its cold hanging weight—the basis for our pricing—was electronically recorded. Each one weighed some fifty pounds, give or take. From the scale, they rolled off into my arms and then out the door to the co-op truck.

Meat trucks ordinarily have rails and hooks enabling carcasses to hang, just like in a cooler. Our truck, though, had no such accoutrements. Its cooler had been built for hauling milk samples to dairy labs, and its construction was much too delicate to have 1,000 pounds of meat dangling from the roof. "What does the regular guy do?" I asked R&E's man.

"He piles 'em on the floor. Throws 'em on that padding."

"You're kidding."

"Keeps his center of gravity low."

"I guess it must," I said. But it seemed unfitting to carry prime meat around as though it were a pile of sausage. Still, there was no other choice. I stacked twenty carcasses on the meat-wagon's floor and set off for the first of several far-flung customers.

I have always believed that there are two main ways to earn money. One way is to create or accomplish things that have inherent value, the other is to buy things cheap and sell them dear. Both of these strategies requires very different skills, and even different character traits. The likelihood of anyone excelling at both creating goods *and* selling them strikes me as just about nil. I like to think of myself as an essentially creative person. Good thing, too—because I found out long ago that I could scarcely sell a box of Christmas cards to my own mother.

But here was a conundrum: I thought I had agreed merely to deliver lambs, but in fact the job entailed *selling* meat to a frosty cadre of retail butchers. I was expected to swap jokes with them, to gladhand and stroke them and goose them into accepting what my sheet plainly asserted they had ordered. For example, one note from the manager read: "East Lick IGA—4 lambs. Find Rodney and ask him how he liked the brains I gave him last week. Would he like some more brains, as a personal favor? I could drop them off next week. Will he up his order to 5 lambs?"

I found the East Lick IGA and pulled the truck around back. I eased up to the unloading dock and climbed onto it. All the doors were locked. I jogged around the back of an entire shopping center, entered the front door like any grocery customer, and strode to the meat section. "Help you?" asked a woman who was hacking chickens into parts.

"I'm looking for Rodney."

"He's not here today."

"Gee, I—well, perhaps you'd know. Did he like his brains?"

"Say what?"

"Brains."

"We don't stock them. Better try the A&P."

"Wait," I said. "I'm not here to *buy* meat. I'm here to *sell* meat. I'm the lamb guy this week."

"You're the what?"

"The lamb. From Yankee Shepherd. I've got the delivery truck out back."

"Oh," she said. "*That.* Hey—Billy." Somebody named Billy came over. He was Rodney's stand-in. We went to the loading dock, and I opened the truck's back door, revealing twenty lambs stacked like corpses in some common grave.

"Only taking two this week," said Billy.

"But—my sheet says four."

"Sorry," he said. "Stuff ain't moving. Not at your price, anyway. We got Western lamb on special."

I shrugged. "I just drive the truck. Just helping out, see? Filling orders. And my order sheet says to give you four."

"*Two.* Hey—take it or leave it, Jack."

"Two—right, two," I agreed cheerfully. But I thought: I think I've heard that line somewhere before. Back before we had a co-op.

Billy pulled his two lambs off the pile and sent me on my way; as the morning wore on, this nightmare got a good deal worse. The next meat manager complained that last week's lambs were tough. Somebody had brought some chops back. Was I going to make a refund? The next meat manager waved an ad for Western lamb at prices far less than ours and cancelled his subscription. Zip. No more. Take *that*, Jack.

I guessed this rough handling must all be a part of selling meat; I guessed that the co-op's regular manager could play the game of give-and-take and come out unbruised, steadily building up his order book. Passing out the odd favor, asking after wives and kids. But by noon, I had a pickup full of unsold lambs and a thin book of drastically curtailed orders for the coming week. And then the Yankee Shepherd truck—our single quasi-asset—began handling very funny. As though bent on self-destruction. Still, I had my rounds to make.

At a busy stoplight in downtown Burlington, a pedestrian stepped from the curb to tap my window. "Front left tire's mighty soft," he told me.

This turned out to be a colossal understatement. I parked and discovered I was driving on a rim. In the nearest service station, an amused mechanic told me I had turned the entire wheel to junk.

"But I'm hauling meat," I said. "I have to sell this stuff or smell it. I can't wait around on this."

"Put your spare on," the mechanic suggested. Sure. I found the spare tire slung beneath the pickup bed, but the suspension system that held it in place had completely frozen up from corrosion and dirt and road-salt. I borrowed a hammer—and a hacksaw and a Vice-Grips, too—and labored underneath the truck to extricate the spare. Forty minutes later, Yankee Shepherd was back on the road. But the Yankee Shepherd meatman was covered in grime and rust.

What to do? Biting the bullet, I stopped at a vast emporium of low-cost consumer goods and bought myself new clothes. New shirt, new socks, new pants—Vermont Lamb ambassadors can't look like grease monkeys, after all. Then I wolfed an Arby's Roast Beef sandwich, for poetic justice. Then I started ambling south to finish up the day's route, unloading the odd lamb and nursing a profound depression.

As for the seven unsold lambs at day's end, the co-op rented cooler space where I hung them pending the manager's return. He returned the next day, fortunately, and showed up for his truck. "Well?" he pumped me. "How'd you make out?"

"Not my line of work," I told him. "I sure hope the co-op can survive my day as meatman."

"Oh, I think we will."

"You make some kind of deal up in Montreal?"

"Maybe."

"Tell me something," I said. "I thought when we got this co-op rolling, we were going to dictate the price of lamb."

"Well, we try. We're gaining on it. Selling meat, though—selling meat has *always* been a cutthroat business. Killer business. So to speak."

"Interesting choice of phrase."

"Well, it's not an easy game. But we're learning how to play it."

"Maybe *you* are." I tossed the manager his keys. "But after yesterday, count me *out* of selling lambs. I'll just grow them for you."

"Fair enough."

He drove off to do battle for the co-op in the rough-and-tumble marts of trade, and I walked off to check my lambing barn and tend a hungry flock. That was half a dozen years ago, already; Yankee Shepherd is still selling lambs, and I'm still growing them. With the benefit of hindsight, it appears we both succeeded.

Pig in a Poke

For me at least, the depressing realities of selling meat have been made more palatable by marketing through a co-op. Most of our lambs, most of the time, are now sold profitably. But the thin margins inherent in meat production did cause me to ponder all conceivable alternatives, and I realized there is one lamb "market" in which sellers truly *can* dictate their price. It happens every time another shepherd—or potential shepherd—goes shopping for breeding stock, the working ewes and rams from which annual crops of lamb and wool are harvested.

Even crossbred lambs, when sold as breeding stock, can bring up to twice their value as meat; purebred sheep with appropriate pedigrees fetch much higher prices. When a good proportion of one's lambs are sold for breeding, the *average* price received per pound can float upward into a monetary comfort zone. And, unlike slaughter lambs shipped off to an abattoir, animals sold for breeding purposes will never trouble a shepherd's conscience—or a shepherd's children—in dark, philosophic moments.

It took several years for me to boost our own flock to its target of eighty ewes, a level at which profits—at least profits on paper—started to look interesting. During this expansion phase, any and all ewe lambs who proved willing to be bred were immediately pressed into service; consequently, I could offer no breeding stock for sale. But the year came when the flock bore sixty ewe lambs, of which I needed only ten to replace old sheep. So I looked forward to making a modest killing—or, indeed, a modest living—by purveying excess females to fellow shepherds at much higher prices than the meat market offered. Once I had the lambs weaned from their mothers' milk, penned, and started on a high-octane "finishing" ration, I took out ads in several farm papers:

EWE LAMBS—PROLIFIC CROSSBREDS, EARLY BREEDERS. OUTSTANDING QUALITY. USE OUR FLOCK RECORDS TO PICK YOUR CHOICE, $150/HEAD.

The telephone didn't quite ring off the hook, but I did get several nibbles and set up appointments to show off my critters. "Aren't you going to choose *your own* replacements first?" asked Cheryl.

"I don't think that's fair—do you?"

"*Fair?*"

"Look—if you went shopping and some breeder said he'd already picked the best lambs for himself, would you buy there?"

"It would depend on what he had for sale."

"But if you *knew* he was holding back the good stuff—"

"Anyone who sells off his very best breeding stock isn't going to be in *that* business for long."

"Think of it as making an investment, though. In advertising. Simple way to make a reputation for ourselves."

"For being crazy?"

"*Shrewd.* Once people see the sort of sheep we're putting on the market, they'll be lining up."

"Are you actually going to hand out our production records?"

"Sure."

"But why?"

"No one buys a pig in a poke, these days. The more hard facts we put on the table, the more confidence our customers will feel—and that counts for something. We can charge more."

"You had better," Cheryl warned. "Because you won't be charging more for long, after setting up competitors in business with our best stock."

Oh, I knew she had a point. We *did* possess some fairly exceptional genetic material, and very few competitors had lambs like ours to offer. When I had first ventured forth to purchase breeding stock, I scoured the Northeast for specimens of a new commercial cross derived from three distinct breeds: Dorset, Rambouillet, and the recently imported Finnish Landrace. Ewes with these bloodlines can be startlingly hypersexed, with very early puberty and excellent prospects for rearing twenty lambs in the course of an eight-year life. Such sheep tend to be selected for prolificacy—for lambing early and often, and for dropping several lambs at once—at the expense of more traditional traits; consequently, they do not suit every shepherd's fancy. But I had made an early wager that these crossbreds would become a basic tool in reviving New England's moribund sheep industry. For a brief, happy moment it looked like I might be right.

Cashing in on my good fortune carried an implicit price: every ewe lamb that I sold for breeding purposes could, in principle, be used against me. If I seemed to have a corner on this unlikely market, surely it would not last long. If I was too proud—or crazy—to sell only second-best, at least it behooved me to insist on getting my price while I could.

I walked to the barn and appraised our situation as though I were a customer come to see my wares. Right away I realized that when one offers breeding stock, one's entire farming operation is on display. The place ought to look neat, even gussied-up; there is no excuse for broken feeders, sagging gates, or giant burdocks sprouting from barnyard manure piles. Such signs of unthrifty farming had become routine components of my field of vision, but they had to be cleaned up in order to exude success. Who would purchase breeding ewes from someone whose farm was visibly decaying?

So I set about various Herculean clean-up and fix-up chores, reflecting that in selling meat-lambs all that had ever mattered was my critters' weight when they climbed aboard a platform scale. No packer had ever asked whether my barn looked neat before setting a price on my lambs; on the other hand, no packer had ever paid me $150 per head. If I could sell forty or fifty ewe lambs at that price, my time spent cleaning up the farm would be well compensated.

I pondered, too, how best to present the production records on my flock so as to tempt a customer. Finally I settled on creating an index card for every single lamb, indicating parentage, number of siblings, recorded weights at thirty-day intervals, average daily gains, and complete veterinary histories. Producing this stack of cards turned into a major project, keeping me up late for several nights running. Once it was accomplished, though, the deck could be shuffled and cut any way one wished: a customer could sort and rank the full group of lambs according to whatever commercial traits were most valued. Certainly, I thought, going to such an effort ought to bring cash rewards.

Came the first customer, a hard-boiled old-timer whose few remaining teeth were mottled and stained with chewing tobacco. I ushered him into the barn and watched him stare at my lamb crop for the longest time. I waited, patient and respectful of his judgment. At length, he told me dryly: "I don't like these sheep."

"You *don't*?" I was shocked—and wounded, too—but I made an effort at bright, engaging conversation. "Now, why would anybody say a thing like that?"

He spat, barely missing one of my prized ewe lambs. "Because there is no meat on them."

"But—but these lambs are bred for multiple births. This is a *ewe* breed, so they're slender—even svelte. But just put the right ram on them, and you'll see some meat-wagons. Guaranteed."

"Tell me, son—have you been at this very long?"

My hard-nosed colleague's ignorance of modern trends in breeding proved impenetrable; I never even got the chance to flash my index cards. But at least I now had the premises cleaned up, and I recognized the need to hone my sales skills. I had to *direct* the conversation with my customers, rather than react defensively to harsh appraisals. I needed a better story, too, about my stock, and I had to learn to tell it unflappably.

My next customer, a middle-aged woman in a handknit cardigan, stopped by a few days later. "The thing about these ewes," I said before we even reached the barn, "is that they're bred for maternal traits, not carcass size. And if you'll just look through these production records—"

"What on earth are those?"

"Every ewe lamb has a card, see? Here's an ear-tag number—R7605—and here it tells you she was born a twin. Twenty-five pounds at thirty days, and on April 10th she got a shot for tetanus, and—look here. An average daily gain of six-tenths of a pound."

"All that really interests me is wool," she told me, handing back the cards with a puzzled smile. "What are their fleeces like?"

"*Nice* fleeces," I assured her. We had gained the barn now, and I led her inside. I caught a lamb and let the woman handle it; she took a wool-card from her bag and tugged at the fleece, pulling off a generous sampling of creamy fibers. Then, while I watched, she took out a magnifying glass to examine these.

"You know," I said, "the key trait in sheep nowadays is lambing percentage—the number of lambs born per ewe per year. When you put twins and triplets in a breeding program, it's like guaranteeing profits down the road."

"I don't like the *crimp* of this wool. Not for handspinning."

"Crimp? But—"

"These sheep aren't what I expected. Sorry to have wasted your time."

There were other customers, too, over the next few weeks, but it is fair to say that none of them were so forward-looking as to value the traits I was offering for sale. I may have been too far ahead of my time; my lambs' time was quickly coming to a close, however. In the lamb-fattening biz, a ewe lamb that has reached 110 pounds is ripe for slaughter and will become *over*ripe if she puts on much more weight. Also, she has reached the age of sexual maturity. Ram lambs penned nearby are apt to be knocking heads over her, rather than eating grain and growing big and strong themselves. One has to fish, or one has to cut bait. In the absence of any willing customers for breeding stock, it was time to think about shipping my lambs for slaughter.

Sensing my growing frustration over this debacle, Cheryl suggested that a market for breeding stock had to be developed slowly, haltingly, with endless patience. Since I had not found a single customer, I at least could save the very best lambs for my own replacements. Then, a couple days before my lambs were booked for slaughter, she told me someone else had called. A whole family, actually, was on their way from Massachusetts to look over my ewe lambs.

I dug my index cards out of the drawer where I had stashed them and shuffled through the deck. The truly superior ewe lambs jumped right out at me: triplets who had grown at the sort of rate one usually finds only in single lambs, with two teats at their sole disposal. Why was no one smart enough to recognize the value represented by these supersheep? Advanced genetic strategies had scared away my customers, and my numbers had confused them. I put the cards away and vowed, this time, to keep my mouth shut.

A couple hours later, looking out a window of my house, I watched two adults and two small girls climb from a station wagon and

head toward the barn. By the time I came to join them, each child had picked out the ewe lamb of her dreams. "These ones are for sale?" asked their father anxiously.

"Absolutely."

"These are awfully pretty lambs," his wife said. "Look at that one's face, there—isn't that just the sweetest expression?"

"She looks really glad to see you," I agreed.

"So—I guess that's three hundred dollars? Would you take a check?"

"Of course. By the way—do you folks have many sheep?"

"Well, we have two now."

"Do you *know* about these sheep?"

"Aren't they the ones that are supposed to have twins and triplets?"

"Right."

"We're just getting started, as you see. We don't know a lot. But this breed makes sense to me—more bang for the buck, right?"

He handed me my first check in the breeding-stock trade, and I helped him load two ewe lambs in the back of his station wagon. They drove off happily, and I went to the house to check my stack of index cards. Based on cold production records, they had bought completely undistinguished lambs for breeding stock. Losers. It was just a tiny sale but I savored victory. I got my price and I managed to keep the best.

Vermont's sheep circles are small and fairly intimate, with gossip being regularly carried from farm to farm by traveling shearers and other entrepreneurs. So I was astonished, just a little while ago, to hear my shearer brag that he had recently acquired a couple of the most prolific sheep in all New England. From a man in Massachusetts, who had bought them as young lambs from guess who?

"Those sheep must be six years old," I told him.

"Yes. But one of them has dropped either *quads or quints* for five years running, and the other's not too far behind."

"Quintuplets?"

"And she *raises* them, too, with a little bit of help. I've had my eye on that pair for a long time. Seed stock. If I can get them to lamb just a few more times, I'll build a flock around their blood."

"Smart idea."

"Tell me—why'd you go and sell off lambs like that?"

"To make a reputation," I ventured. "And I *did*, huh?"

"I don't think so. *He* did."

"Those weren't any special lambs. I still have the data on them. Those folks never asked to see my record cards, anyway."

"*You* have any ewes dropping quints, year after year?"

"Not a one."

"Then maybe I can sell you some better stock, someday."

Farm Tours

Thirty-odd years ago, when I was growing up in South Jersey, my fifth-grade class took a field trip to a locally famous farm, the Walker-Gordon Dairy. This innovative operation had built an impressive machine dubbed The Rotolactor—a huge, heavy, slowly turning carousel onto which cows marched for their twice-daily milkings. The point was to show suburban kids that milk comes from cows, but perhaps I was not alone in learning the false lesson that it takes a merry-go-round to get the stuff to flow. Had I been a little older, I might have observed that a Rotolactor represents a near-comic excess of ingenuity applied to a relatively simple problem and might be regarded more as an exuberant psychocultural artifact than as the sort of invention that necessity is known to mother.

But there are many ways to tour someone else's farm and leave with false impressions, and nowadays I remind myself of this several times each year when one busload of school kids or another pulls up the driveway to tour ours. I have created nothing so astonishing as a Rotolactor, but in children's eyes the sheer drama of barnyard life can easily obscure the lesson I would have them learn: that shepherding represents the artful exploitation of each sheep's ability to produce both food and fiber, bleating lambs as well as wool.

Children are more apt to learn different truths, however. The one product they invariably watch getting produced on the spot is manure, and school groups of a certain age can become obsessed with the ubiquity of fecal matter to the exclusion of any further observation. Somewhat more disturbing is when visitors get fixated on abstruse philosophic issues, such as whether my sheep are *happy*. I perform a hundred chores—some very large, some minuscule—to provide a measure of comfort and security for my woolly charges, which after all is in my manifest self-interest. But their abstract happiness—or, put negatively, their existential plight—seems hardly my affair.

On one of the first occasions when I exposed my flock to visitors, the tour group consisted of a youth club sponsored by the local Humane Society. These kids had a firm agenda, and it didn't take them long to turn up putative evidence of animal unhappiness. "What did you do to those lambs' tails?" demanded a strident nine-year-old.

"I, ah, cut those off. Like in the nursery rhyme—remember? Little Bo-Peep?"

"*Why*?"

Now, there are many reasons for cutting off the tails of lambs, and I labored to explain a few of these to my guests. Cleanliness. Carcass merit. Breeding efficiency. Just as I had a few small heads nodding in agreement, a grown-up chaperone asked pointedly: "But does it *hurt* them?"

I took a deep breath. "Well, I imagine that it does," I answered truthfully. "But not for long."

"How would *you* know?"

"I suppose I wouldn't. But it doesn't seem to bother them *too* much, and the wound heals quickly. It may be—unpleasant. But I think these lambs are better off for it in the long run."

"Do you give them anaesthesia?" asked a young animal-rights activist.

"Oh, no. Not for docking tails."

"Why not?"

"It just isn't done. It wouldn't be, um, cost-effective."

And there I had my foot in it, for sure. By the time I had

explained what *cost-effective* meant, as applied to this arena of torture and dismemberment, the good shepherd had metamorphosed in their eyes into some cruel sadist. And then, heading out the door, some lucky child tripped over a bucket of amputated tails.

"Eeek!"

"Gross!"

"Yuck! Let's get out of here."

I could be misunderstood but not, of course, censured for observing recommended practices in husbandry. I lived to host more tours. A year or so later—when Ethan was in kindergarten—an entire yellow school bus filled with his classmates came to tour the barn toward the end of lambing season. It was the sort of scene a shepherd loves to share: a hundred-odd newborns were romping in assorted pens while their moms looked on, bemused. But I was hopeful, too, that one older sheep—a ewe who had been in and out of labor all night long—might deliver her babies in time for this impressionable crowd to witness the miracle of birth.

Sure enough, the lady-in-waiting was presenting two small feet when I led these eager children into the barn. Given the advanced stage of her labor and my high regard for this ewe's maternal instinct, I felt no hesitation at giving a tug or two to aid the lamb's delivery. Seconds later, to a chorus of oohs and aahs, there lay the dripping newborn on a nest of yellow straw, dead as a doornail. From external signs I judged it had been dead in utero, for several days perhaps.

"Ick!" said one young visitor.

"Uh-oh," said a little girl.

"Looks pretty nearly dead," said one extremely frank child.

"Gosh," I told the crowd of assembled children. "This lamb appears to be extremely weak."

"Can't you *do* something?" asked their distraught teacher.

I picked the lamb up, showmanlike, and began administering mouth-to-mouth resuscitation. I sucked salty fluids from its airway and spat them out. I gave its little chest a gentle cardiac massage—but there's only so much one can do with a dead lamb before even hopeful kids will recognize it's dead. "This lamb is *so* weak," I said, "perhaps we ought to just leave it here and—"

"Look—here comes another one!"

The ewe lay on her side and groaned and squirted out another lamb—again without the faintest ghost of a vital sign. Dead. Dead. "This doesn't happen around here very often," I offered lamely, but by now the teacher and several parent-chaperones and even the bus driver were herding the children toward more lively corners of the barn. I joined them, too, leaving my confused ewe to lick and paw these lifeless fruits of her ripe womb. The kids proved rather more adept than grown-ups at transferring their interest from obstetric nightmares to happier subjects. But after ten minutes of answering their questions, I excused myself to go back and check on the ewe.

Lo and behold, she had delivered herself of two *more* lambs—both thoroughly alive and already struggling to their feet, wobbling toward their mother's faucets. I almost shouted, but I squelched it as a crafty inspiration came to mind. I ditched the two dead babies where the visitors would never find them, then called Ethan's classmates back to share the good news. "These newborn lambs are doing *much* better now," I told them. "I can't even think when I've seen such a recovery."

They ran to see, and I learned how it feels to be regarded as one who can raise the dead. Only the bus driver—a fellow farmer, doubtless—seemed unfooled, but he was kind enough not to blow this for me. One week later, the local newspaper reported on the wonderful field trip that let kids "get to see two lambs actually come into the world." Make that four, I thought, sighing with relief.

Emboldened by my growing prowess as a farm-tour guide, I started unabashedly planning show-biz elements of flock management to coincide with scheduled visits from nursery schools, day-care centers, and the like. Moving the flock from one pasture to another can be one such dramatic focus, given that I have trained my sheep, using Pavlovian methods, to come running anytime I clap my hands. Watching ewes get shorn can be an equally arresting experience for visitors. The most colorful sight I ever showed a group of kids, however, was a green lamb. *Bright* green. And in unveiling this surprise exhibit, I experienced the ultimate tour-guide thrill: the moment when the leader himself learns something new and different.

In a sheep flock bred for prolificacy, in which many ewes each year drop triplets, much depends on getting sheep to raise lambs born to other moms. When a twin lamb dies—for any reason—the shepherd grabs a triplet and uses one of several tricks to get the bereaved mother to accept it as her own; shepherds call this process *grafting*. A peerless method is to skin the dead lamb and dress the graftee in that woolly suit. Since ewes initially identify their offspring by sense of smell, the "skin-grafted" lamb utilizes a mother's surest instinct to fake her into offering affection. And milk, too.

On our farm, we "skin-graft" a few lambs every year; it always works at first, but the moment of truth comes when we pull the dead skin *off* and see what sort of maternal bond has been created. It's a gamble choosing exactly when to do this: if the bond is *only* skin-deep, the graft will be lost. On the other hand, a skin-suit that begins to rot in place becomes counterproductive for all parties concerned. Thirty-six hours is the average length of time that we have come to settle on, as a protocol. But recently, knowing that a school group was coming to the farm and wanting to leave them with a memorable impression, I let a lamb wear another's skin for three days straight. And then, in the presence of twenty-seven youngsters, I took a sharp knife and unzipped it, so to speak.

"Whooeee!"

"Jesum crow!"

"Look at that! That lamb's turned *green!*"

"Gosh," I said. "I've never seen this before."

The lamb was very green, indeed. Nearly *iridescent* green. Some sort of algal growth had found its way underneath the sheepskin coat and, helped by damp and humid weather, it had taken root in the lamb's own wool. Apart from this bright flora, the lamb appeared healthy. I had always wondered whether a foster mother, having used her nose to accept a grafted lamb, might yet be dissuaded by conflicting visual evidence; now we would all find out. This lamb undoubtedly looked different from anything a mother might expect. With bated breath, I placed it back into the newborns' pen.

Mother didn't bat an eyelash. The lamb ducked beneath her belly, grabbed a teat, and started nursing; the ewe showered its emerald derrière with sloppy kisses.

"What can you do with a lamb like that?" a child asked me.

I decided not to bat an eyelash, either. "Makes a *perfect* Irish stew," I answered. And that was that.

Green lambs, tortured lambs, dead lambs raised to bleating life— I have given plenty of kids uncertain food for thought. Still, the tour groups come, as though my lambing barn had found its way onto the map. As though I had built some sort of Rotolactor to show off. What do children *really* learn by going on a farm visit? I suppose that's their own business. I confess I'd hate to know.

Manure Happens

In the modern world, livestock barns are nearly always built with careful forethought as to how they will be cleaned. A system of floor gutters and steel paddles may shuffle manure automatically to a holding tank or spreader; at the very least, barn doors are built wide enough to admit tractors equipped with end-loaders and scraper blades. Farmers have had plenty of occasion, down the centuries, to consider better ways of dealing with manure. A barn's design can thus become a triumph of human ingenuity over backache.

Not *my* barns, however. As an urban refugee who moved to Vermont in the early 1970s, the farm buildings I erected paid more attention to classic lines and shapely masses than to such mundane concerns as where my sheep's manure would go and what would happen to it once it got there. Where it went was on the floor, mixing in with bedding and unpalatable stems of hay to make a hard, dry pack that deepened with each passing day. Over weeks and months and years, the floor rose up to greet the ceiling. Headroom dwindled steadily.

The first of my several barns was just 600 square feet in size—no big deal—and I built it the year of Ethan's birth, 1976. Five years later, in honor of the birth of Anaïs, I cleaned that barn down to bare concrete with a five-tine pitchfork. In those days I owned an antique manure spreader, but it fell apart toward the end of this Herculean labor. After that—since 1981—I let the "bed-pack" in that little barn build up unthwarted. It was never hard to find a reason, any given day, to put off such a cleaning chore. In time, we used the little barn only at the peak of spring lambing season, and I trained myself to duck beneath its threatening rafters anytime I entered it.

Things changed recently, though, when 10-year-old Anaïs acquired a pony twice her age. This beast needed a stall, and the little barn seemed an ideal place to put one...except for the three-foot depth of dried manure and bedding heaped across its floor. The pony would have been reduced to crawling on its knees. I told Anaïs I would help her build an official horse stall if she'd help me clean the barn.

"Sure," she answered innocently. I unearthed our collection of old pitchforks, and we set to work together. Half an hour later, she began expressing second thoughts. Breaking chunks of crusted dung free from the compacted mass and heaving them into the nearby pickup truck had already raised a blister on her slender, childish hands. And we had scarcely made a dent in the broad, deep sea before us. Luckily, Anaïs's brother stopped by the barn to see what we were up to. "Want to help?" his sister begged him.

Ethan hefted a manure fork, nodded with determination, and pitched in. With three of us working together, we could make manure fly. I showed the kids how to tease the upper bed-pack off in shallow, pizza-sized, manageable layers; once its desiccated surface had been stripped away, the damp material beneath proved rather more tractable. Still, by the time Cheryl came to check our progress, Ethan had decided that this kind of work should be worth money. "Don't they have a law about the minimum wage?" he asked. "And about child labor?"

"Do they?" I scratched my head. "Gosh, I never heard of any—"

"Two bucks an hour," Cheryl proposed, to my shock and fear of serious impoverishment. When I made a face, she added: "To be paid upon completion."

The kids thought that sounded like a pretty good deal, and Cheryl made out time-sheets for them. Over the next three weeks they put in thirty hours with me. Each. We huffed and puffed together, swapping lies and singing along with the radio. A growing patch of concrete floor was getting steadily exposed, though nothing near the size of a horse stall. On our fourth Saturday afternoon, I sensed their enthusiasm dampening steadily. I paused to get the mail. There, in a farmers' paper, I read that the University of Vermont had started offering a *manure testing service.* "Look at this!" I told the kids, waving the advertisement.

"Test manure for *what?*" asked Ethan.

"Nitrogen, phosphorus, potassium—the same nutrients we buy in pelleted fertilizer. This is free, though."

"You mean this manure's worth money?"

"Maybe we should get it tested—then we'd know for sure." I knew, of course, that our manure had fertilizer value. But after having sat around for up to ten years, I was curious as to how much value might be left. And having a sample of our dunghill laboratory-tested seemed a clever way to keep my kids engaged in a chore that was fast coming to seem poorly compensated. And spiritually unfulfilling.

So, next day, I drove to the office of our county's Agricultural Extension Service. An agent had me fork over twenty-five dollars—no small sum—for a Manure Test Kit. The kit consisted of a one-quart plastic jar and a form on which I would "describe my situation" with respect to manure. I took it home to let the kids help me fill it out.

"*How is manure loaded?*" I read. "They give us four choices—*Pump, Gravity, Barn Cleaner, Other.*"

"Am I like a Barn Cleaner?" Ethan asked.

"No—that's a machine. I think you're like an Other." So we wrote down: *Other—Children (2).*

"What's next?" asked Anaïs.

"*Manure Incorporation into Soil.*"

"What does that mean?"

"How long our manure lies on the ground before we work it in. *Same Day as Spread, Next Day, 3 to 5 Days*—"

"Better put *Forever,*" said my son.

"We call that *Topdressing.* It *does* sink in, over time, but some of the nitrogen gets lost into the air. All right—let's go fill this jar."

Heading for the barn, I tried to acquaint my kids with the vagaries of collecting a reliable sample. By my reckoning, the barn held twenty *tons* of old manure; we were going to choose scarcely a pound for chemical analysis—a mere forty-thousandth of the total bed-pack. "Whatever goes into that jar has got to represent the whole," I explained soberly. "Otherwise the test will stink."

"This test is going to stink pretty bad, anyway," Anaïs fired back.

"Is this like 'garbage in, garbage out?' " laughed Ethan.

"I have an idea," I said. "Let's *each* choose our own sample. Then we can mix them up and take a sample out of *that*." It struck them as a perfectly sensible solution, so we took our pitchforks and carefully teased at the exposed faces of manure, searching for appealing samples. Ethan chose a section of thin, brittle, fibrous top-crust—because, as he said, it reminded him of plywood. Anaïs chose a damp mud-ball from directly off the concrete floor, where it had probably been composting since her birth. Then, to round out our sample, I chose a green-veined wad of gunk from the middle of the pile—vintage 1987, roughly. We stirred all these up in a five-gallon pail, then chose a quart to send off to the university. Using a garden trowel, I packed it into the plastic jar.

"It says here you're supposed to freeze the sample," said Ethan, reading from the sheet of printed instructions.

"It *does*?"

"'Do this immediately after collecting the sample to prevent the loss of ammonia-N, keeping the sample frozen until delivery to the lab.'"

"That must be for dairy farmers spreading fresh manure each day," I countered. "This manure has had a *lot* of time to lose ammonia."

"It says right here that you're supposed to freeze it."

Never one to teach my kids to disrespect authority, I gave them time off work to carry our manure sample up to the kitchen and stash it in a quiet little corner of the freezer. And that's where Cheryl found it several days later, looking for the Ben and Jerry's. "Hey," she hollered. "What's in here?"

"You don't want to know," I said. But not before the kids had told her it was our manure sample.

"*What* manure sample?"

"From the little barn. We're going to have it analyzed."

"What's it doing in my freezer?"

"We're just trying to follow the instruc—"

"Get it out of here." Cheryl opened the kitchen door and placed our precious sample on the back porch. I could hardly blame her.

"But it's not supposed to thaw," said Ethan.

"Better hope for frost, then."

Next day, I arranged my schedule to deliver our somewhat-thawed sample to the university. No problem—I watched the lab technician log it in, then place it in an ordinary refrigerator. The white-coated man was enthusiastic about manure. His lab had tested forages and soils and feed grains for decades, but only in the past year had they launched this bold new venture into dung. By giving farmers better information about manure, chemical fertilizers could be used in a wiser, more environmentally sound fashion.

"So—how many samples have come in?" I asked, trying to share his glee.

"Thirteen—you're the fourteenth. First *sheep* sample, too."

It didn't sound like a revolution in the making. I went home and watched the mail for the next couple weeks, and soon enough I opened my Manure Analysis Report. "Look at this," I showed the kids. "Sixteen pounds of nitrogen per ton. And eighteen pounds of phosphorus. And thirty-eight pounds of potash."

"Is that a lot?" Anaïs asked. "I thought a ton meant two thousand pounds."

"Doesn't sound like much," scoffed Ethan.

I switched on my mental calculator. Down at the local Agway store, nitrogen was selling for twenty-eight cents per pound. Phosphorus was twenty-four cents, and potassium was sixteen. My well-aged manure had a cash value of nearly fifteen dollars per ton.

"In that case I want a raise," said Ethan.

"What for?"

"You said twenty tons, right? So cleaning that barn is like giving you three hundred dollars."

I could see he had a point. I also saw we had a lot of bed-pack yet to move, and I wasn't keen on doing it alone. "Maybe you kids would like to work for a contract price?"

"How much?"

"If I let you split three hundred dollars, I'd break even—right?"

"Deal!" they cried eagerly.

"But you have to *finish*."

They set off for the barn, counting riches in each cubic foot.

Today, a few months later, Anaïs's pony has a first-class stall, with concrete floor and Dutch doors and more than ample headroom. The little barn is back in service. Manure is happening once again—horse manure, as yet untested by our university. But my daughter faithfully cleans it out each several days. She has seen the consequences of letting small problems pile into three-foot dunghills. She's too smart to let that happen. And if Anaïs ever sets out to build a barn, my hunch is it will be designed with chores firmly in mind.